# The Boy in the Suitc

## Holocaust Family Stories of Survival

Sheryl Needle Cohn

*To Diane that you're keeping these memories Alive & for your for all these years*

**Hamilton Books**

A member of
The Rowman & Littlefield Publish
*Lanham • Boulder • New York • Toronto*

**Copyright © 2012 by**
**Hamilton Books**
4501 Forbes Boulevard
Suite 200
Lanham, Maryland 20706
Hamilton Books Acquisitions Department (301) 459-3366

Estover Road
Plymouth PL6 7PY
United Kingdom

Library of Congress Control Number: 2011936239
ISBN: 978-0-7618-5705-1 (clothbound : alk. paper)
ISBN: 978-0-7618-5706-8 (paperback : alk. paper)
eISBN: 978-0-7618-5707-5

*Euromap. Courtesy of Graphicmaps.com + city & shtetl edits by author (snc).*

# Contents

*Contents*

# Foreword

It is important to continue to tell the stories of those brutally humiliated, tortured, and murdered during the Holocaust. Those innocent victims who survived this unthinkable trauma will soon be gone. One noble last form of resistance is the courage of survivors and their second and third generation children in sharing their stories with Holocaust historian, Sheryl Needle Cohn.

Sheryl's own paternal family stories are told in Chapters One and Two of this book. It is through the Belorussian chapter that the author and I share the anger of the past, message of the Shoah in the present, and hope of the future. The systematic, murderous Nazi regime and their collaborators continued the long oppression of the Jewish people in the Shtetls of Europe and the Russian territories.

In 1941, as Sheryl's relatives were being shot in ditches in Dubno and Lyhakovichi, my father and uncles, with guns in hand, were keeping Jews alive in the forests of Belorussia. The Bielski Brothers engaged in the ultimate defiance, stay alive, fight back, and live to tell the world of these horrors. The murder of their own family members and innocent Jews led them to become notorious and heroic armed partisans, as seen in the movie *Defiance*.

Sheryl's act of defiance in writing this book ensures that the innocent victims will no longer remain anonymous in their deaths. As the Maggid of her ancestral Dubno before her, Sheryl tells unique and inspirational stories in her book. In doing so, she honors the memory of the brave resistors, rescuers, and especially the families whose ultimate revenge is their continuance today.

Sincerely, *ZB*
Zvi Bielski, son of the notorious commander Zus Bielski of the
Bielski Brothers Brigade.
December 28, 2010

# Acknowledgments

This book is dedicated to my grandma Bella, if not for her courage and wisdom, I would not even exist. Thank you to the survivors and their adult children, and to the families of brave resistance fighters who stood up against the tyranny of Nazism. Your trust in sharing your stories with me is humbling.

Thank you to the many Holocaust agencies, organizations, and museums worldwide. Thank you to the extraordinary worldwide network of hidden child survivors, and second generation organizations, from whom information and contacts were often just an internet click away. Thank you, spasibo and gracias to UCF volunteer research assistants Jennifer, Marina and Mariela for their domestic and international work. Thanks Barbara, Susanne, and Behic for your excellent proofreading and frankness, after all these years you still keep it real. Thank you to the Jewish community of Sosua, Dominican Republic, and the Perdomo Family for your help and warm hospitality during my stay in your country. Thank you to the south Belgium township of Quaregnon. To Willy Thomas, Michele Messine, and especially Jerry and Marcelle (Micke) Gimborn-Destrain, Merci Beaucoup!

Special thanks to Ms. Shainna Ali, my research assistant and after two productive years, my friend, for her dedication to this project and her continued support in the publication of this book.

Thank you sisters of Phi Alpha Pi: Donna, Big Shelley, Little Shelley and our dearly missed friend Sue. It is almost incredulous to think with your love and support over 45 years I could go from Social Director to Holocaust scholar and author.

I am very grateful to the administrators, faculty, technical and support staff, and my students at the University of Central Florida for allowing me to expand the diversity of my faculty role and to grow professionally.

# Introduction

"When The Last Survivor Is Gone, Who Will Tell of the Holocaust"

Etunia Bauer Katz, survivor

I am not a Holocaust expert; the more I read and research, the less I realize I know. This may sound like a surprising introduction to a book I hope is read by many, but it is the way I sometimes feel. The task of telling the stories of survivors and their families has been daunting at times. Yet I am riding along a river that continues to take me to places I could not have imagined four years ago.

The etiology and original title of my book, "Connecting with the Holocaust," began in 2006, when I discovered genealogical information about my paternal family. As you will read in chapters 1 and 2, my family came from the Russian territories. My beloved grandmother Bella and her parents survived the harsh Russian pogroms in Dubno. My grandfather Max and his family came from the Russian village, shtetl in Yiddish, of Lyakhovichi. Who knew this was actually Belorussia, now Belarus? I certainly did not. And so I thought the story would end here. I planned a trip to my ancestral homelands, with the explicit goal of Walking in the Footsteps of My Grandparents. In July 2006, I had no idea I was about to actually begin an extension of my career as an educator, to that of a Holocaust scholar. You will read how after living in the former Russian territories and in Eastern Europe, my objective was now to Walk in the footsteps of the Holocaust.

Upon return to America, I resumed my life as a college professor, supervising student teacher interns for the University of Central Florida. I asked my interns and their supervising teachers what they knew and taught about the Holocaust to their K-12 students. The scarcity of resources and information in many of their classes greatly concerned me. So I became a resource for my students, which is what good instructors do all the time. But this time, it was also personal. I was invited to speak to organizations and schools in several central Florida counties. I was chosen to study in 2008 at the prestigious International Holocaust School at Yad Vashem, Israel, furthering my status as a Holocaust scholar.

As I would address various groups at speaking engagements, people would come up to me afterwards and share their personal family stories with me. During one of my aptly entitled power-point presentations of Walking in the footsteps of the Holocaust, to a genealogy society, I noticed a woman softly crying. At the conclusion, she approached me and began telling me her story as a Holocaust survivor. Following subsequent speaking engagements, others would tell me their parents were survivors, and the stories began to collect in my consciousness. I would awake at all hours and jot notes, which later I would Google search, then further research, using a multitude of academic and organizational sources. It became clear, that the only way I could ever sleep through the night again, would be to share these stories with interested readers.

I could no longer rely on the occasional public speaking at Shoah remembrances to keep these stories alive. The book you are about to read is not just about my disruptive sleep, but more importantly, it is an homage to the intelligence, courage, and survival of the families in each chapter. Please join me on my river of life journey, as we connect with the Holocaust through *The Boy in the Suitcase: Holocaust Family Stories of Survival.*

"For whoever listens to a witness becomes a witness."
Elie Wiesel

*Chapter One*

# Dubno: From Russian Pogroms to the Holocaust

In 2006 I decided to walk in the footsteps of my paternal grandparents. I journeyed to Dubno, the former Russian shtetl (village) of my grandmother Bella Bittelman Needle. I started out in Kiev, heading west across the Ukraine. My first historical encounter with the city of Lvov showed a once thriving place of Jewish culture and commerce. Subsequent research during the Nazi occupation revealed Ukrainian collaborators beating a young man to the ground. The man was nicely attired in dark slacks, a tailored shirt, and a sports jacket. He looked like he could be a medical student in any twentieth century city. The Ukrainian police under the watchful eye of a Nazi soldier, continued to kick and attack the man, who's apparent crime was being a Jew. Yet both the Polish and Ukrainian police, and other similar Ukrainian archival photos and data show all these people being of the same race and nationality: white, Polish or Ukrainian, born in Lvov, or Dubno. How could the church you enter be cause for your elimination from a cultured twentieth century society? This question continues to plague students of the Holocaust. The Nazi German government from 1933-1945, under Hitler's rule launched the most impressive propaganda campaign against the Jews. Convincing the populace that Judiasm was a race and pestilence needing elimination in order for eastern and western Europe under the mighty German empire to flourish.

My grandmother's village is now located in the western Ukraine. Dubno has always remained in the same area of the world, but which country came after its name was dependent on who conquered and occupied it. The village changed hands from the control of Polish, Russian, and eventually Ukrainian monarchies. During the 16th century the Polish monarchy under King Ostrofski recruited Jews from the Mideast region for their skills as scholars, merchants, and farmers. The king had Jews as tutors for his children and as advisers on financial issues. So for decades Jews lived in the region peacefully and prospered. Later Dubno was taken over by czarist Russia. The czar initiated a series of pogroms that would restrict life for the Jews in the area. Land formerly owned by Jews was now property of the state. Jewish children were restricted from attending public schools, and taxes were levied the on the Jewish population. By the 19th century control of Dubno reverted back to the Polish government. Jewish culture flourished once again and so did the beginning of the communist and Zionist movements in Eastern Europe.

During the governmental transitions over the centuries, although existence was hard in the shtetl, the Bittelman family continued to make a good life for themselves. Their house was located at 22 Rezenicka, Dubno, Russia. David Bittleman, my grandmother's father taught at the local synagogue. Rifka, grandma's mother, bore four children of which my grandmother was one of three girls. At age 13 during the Russian pogroms, Bella's father made arrangements for her to travel to New York City to begin a new life in a new country.

It was a difficult and scary journey, but in 1906 she was met at Ellis Island by Uncle Lou, Rifka's brother. Grandma Bella rolled cigars on the lower Eastside in Uncle Lou's novelty and cigar store to be able to send money back to the old country and get her siblings to New York city. The last person grandma

*Bella Bittelman age 13. Courtesy of snc.*

could get out of the shtetl was her brother Arthur, who in 1935 was in the Zionist Youth Movement, in Dubno, Poland. My one act play *Bella's Story from Pogrom to Holocaust* (2009) chronicles the Bittelman family story, and unfortunately the sad and disturbing murder of the remaining family members. Unfortunately, it is also the sad ending and total destruction of the Jewish community of Dubno and approximately 3,000 other Jewish shtetls.

The ancient city of Dubno was founded by Prince Ostrozky in the 12th century. Dubno is in the Volhynia region of the Ukraine. Konstantin Ostrogski built a castle on the banks of the Ikva River in 1492. Jews are recorded as having arrived in the area early in the 16th century, purchasing land and cattle. A headstone uncovered in the old Jewish cemetery was dated 1581. Jewish town councils and a synagogue were all established, keeping with Jewish law and tradition. However, old traditions of Jews being chased from lands and murdered continued in this region. A peasant and Cossack uprising, the Chmielnicki uprising, resulted in the seizure of homes and land, and the death of approximately 2,000 Dubnovian Jews. They were buried as martyrs outside the eastern synagogue wall.

The Jewish community returned to Dubno in the late 17th century, welcomed back by a new Polish monarchy. In 1780, they briefly abandoned Dubno, fleeing into the woods, due to the plague. The church blamed the Jews for the plague, since they did not succumb to the illness due to hygienic religious laws, once again fostering antisemitism. Upon return, the community thrived and became the hub of commerce and culture. Jakob, the Maggid of Dubno, the ancient traveling teacher and storyteller was the rock star of his time. Doctors, poets, writers, printers, all settled in Dubno. The great annual fair was even moved from Lvov to Dubno for many years. By the late 19th century, approximately 7,000 Jews were living in Dubno. Finally by the early 1900s, the town entered the industrial age with the advent of the very successful Grain and Hops factories.

However, from 1905 through 1918, under Tsarist Russian rule, the Jews of Dubno and the surrounding shetls were subject to often violent pogroms. It was during this period that immigration to America increased, bringing one Bella Bittelman at age 13 to NYC. World War I brought economic hardships to Eastern Europe and the Polish-Russian-Ukrainian territories. The German soldiers did not appear threatening to the Jews, as they had other pressing needs. Things quieted from 1921-1938 in Dubno, once again under Polish governance. In 1931, there were approximately 7400 Jews in the town of 12,700, or fifty-eight percent of the population. Ten small shuls (synagogues) and one grand synagogue, plus a Yiddish theater marked the growing Jewish presence. Every Thursday the main town marketplace bustled with merchants, shoppers, entertainment. Intellectuals studied in secular and religious schools with the hopes of professional future careers. Political groups also formed with Zionist and Communist foci. My great uncle Arthur, Bella's youngest sibling, was a member of the Zionist Youth Movement. While studying in the International School for Holocaust Education in Jerusalem, I excitedly discovered a group photograph of my uncle surrounded by his Zionist friends. It was in the Dubno Memorial Book, one of several shtetl Yizkor (remembrance) books in the archives at Yad Vashem, Israel.

Exchanges between NY and Dubno via postcards and letters and word from emigrating friends and family indicated the change in government in Germany from a democracy to fascism under Hitler's Nazi socialist party. Bella sent money back home and got her sister Anna to America. Dubnovian Jews had survived pogroms over the centuries, and encountered German soldiers before. There was a widespread disbelief that things could be any worse. The expectation seemed to be that German WW II soldiers could not be any worse than their fathers from WWI. Many Jews saw no imminent need to leave their homeland. My Uncle Arthur, being a Zionist, wanted to go to Palestine, then under British control, to rebuild the land of Israel and live on a kibbutz. This troubled my Grandma Bella so she worked extra hours rolling cigars in the cigar factory to save more money. Bella, Anna, and her husband Max made enough money to pay for their brother's immigration to America. Arthur Bittelman would be the last of their family to leave Dubno.

In September 1939, Poland was partitioned by Germany and Russia under the Molotov-Ribbentrop Pact. Hitler controlled the west, and Stalin controlled the east. Jews were now trapped between two dictators, and antisemitic Poles and Ukrainians. WWII economic hardships and a well designed antisemitic campaign from Berlin to vilify the Jews in the region were turning ugly. On September 17, the Russians arrested leaders of the Zionist party. The Soviet state took possession, "Nationalized" Jewish lands and businesses. A public soup kitchen was allowed to continue operating, one which my Great Aunt Anna, Bella's sister had worked during past pogroms.

As western Poland, especially Warsaw was destroyed; Jews that could flee east arrived with horrible stories of murder and ghetto camps. From 1939-1941, covert Nazi infiltrators were arriving in the region to begin working with local police and government workers, like postal carriers, setting the stage for the horrors to follow. Then in June, 1941, Operation Barbarossa, the attack on the Soviet Union by Germany, successfully led to the occupation of the eastern regions. Some families thought this too would be over soon, and the Germans would go through Dubno, further into Russia. Mrs.Kesler, a shtetl mother, packed sandwiches and sent her son Michael and his sister into the woods for the weekend. They would not return, surviving by heading east. Some Jewish Dubnovians were able to escape east into the Soviet

Union, working and fighting against the Germans with the Russians. Many men and women became resistance fighting partisans, hiding in the woods to rescue friends and family. Zvi Maler, a 19 year old engineer, fought with the Soviets against the Germans. Then he made his way to Palestine, Eretz Israel (land of Israel), rescuing fleeing European Jews and bringing them to the new Ein Hararesh Kibbutz in Hadera. He worked as the kibbutz meteorologist and was the patriarch of the Dubnovian Society in Israel until his death in 2009.

June 25, 1941, roving troops of Nazis called Einsatzgruppen, along with Ukrainian local collaborators killed the first group of communist Jewish leaders in Dubno. On July 22, 1941, David Bittelman, Bella's father, was teaching in the synagogue when he was removed by gunpoint. Bella's remaining sister Beila, her husband, children, and cousins were marched past the marketplace to the old Jewish cemetery, ordered to dig large ditches, and then were shot, falling into their own graves.

By August 1941, two "ghetto camps" were established by the Nazis in Dubno. Jews living in secular areas of town were "relocated" to the camps on the outskirts. This forced multiple families to move in with relatives and strangers in crowded apartments and houses. Many possessions left behind, including their homes, were taken by their gentile neighbors. One camp served as a labor camp, where Jews worked outside the ghetto on daily work details. The other camp was strictly for containment. It was in this latter camp that the The Dratwer family was placed. Anna and her family lived in an

*Jews shot in the woods Rovno oblast. Courtesy of United States Holocaust Memorial Museum http://www.ushmm.org.*

*Bittelman Cousins most murdered in Dubno old Jewish cemetery. Courtesy of snc.*

apartment in the center of town, right near the chocolate shop on Aleksandro-
wicz Street. She attended the local school with her Christian friends. One day
an Einsatzgruppe entered the classroom and asked, "Is anyone here a Jew?"
Innocently, Anna's friend pointed to her, not realizing the consequences. The
rear of the camp abutted the Ikva River. The children in Dubno loved swimming in the river on hot summer days. My grandma Bella used to cast pieces
of challah bread upon the Ikva River during the autumn Jewish holiday of
Tashlikh, celebrated during Rosh Hashanah. Now, under the cover of darkness, Anna's mother told her to run into the woods, and never look back. Her
family was too old and weak to escape, but Anna being 16 years old, had a
chance to survive. She climbed out the back window facing the Ikva River,
under the muddy wood, barbed wire fence, following the river bend toward
the forest, never looking back. Partisans were waiting for her, and she eventually made her way to a Swiss orphanage and then to Israel after the war.
The camp was liquidated shortly thereafter. Her mother's selfless actions and
Anna's courage produced the next generations of children and grandchildren.
Anna Dratwer, now Emma Pritel lives on a kibbutz outside of Jerusalem. Her
son Humi Pritel is a coordinator of the Dubno Society in Israel.

    On October 5, 1942, a German engineer named Fritz (Hermann) Graebe,
was asked by one of his Jewish workers to come with him to a killing field

in Dubno. Herr Graebe had been asked by Berlin to take over the engineering firm and factory of Jewish professionals in Dubno. The goal was to modernize the area and build rails for Germany. According to Graebe's testimony at the Nuremberg Trials (Oct'45 & July'46) truckloads of people began arriving and SS guards with dogs and whips ordered the people to undress, pile their clothes to the side, line up at the ditch edge, and were shot and murdered. There is a famous photo from Rovno, the oblast (province) of Dubno, of a woman holding a child, and the guard is ordered to save ammunition by shooting two Jews with one bullet. There are just a few stories of survival, such as children who were buried under their dead parents crawling out of the ditch with minor wounds and escaping to waiting partisans hidden in the forest. Graebe, after seeing these atrocities, organized an escape train for his workers, saving many lives at great risk to himself. After returning to Berlin, due to death threats on himself and his family, Jewish partisans arranged for his safety in America.

A theology student and subsequent Presbyterian minister, Doug Huneke, wrote of this event in his book *The Moses of Rovno*. He wanted to understand why some would put themselves at risk to help others, while others were bystanders, or worse, collaborators. In Graebe's case, it may have helped that his own younger brother was physically disabled, subject to humiliation, and in need of help from others. Perhaps this sense of empathy allowed Fritz to be sensitive and willing to take action to assist others. Mr.Graebe was honored as Righteous Among the Nations by Yad Vashem.

In July 2006 I walked in the footsteps of my grandmother. The Grand Synagogue was a condemned building, but Dubno Society donor funds are helping restore it. Fort Dubno still exists, with the Ikva River behind it. It houses a small museum now. The town historian, Tamara, took me to five memorial killing fields. The Chabad organization in Kiev is protecting the mass murdered remains of approximately 8,000 Jewish victims in these locations:

1. Killing Field One: Old Jewish Cemetery near marketplace ( Bittelman murders)
2. Killing Field Two: Hill-Top (Shibennaya Hill) overlooking lower farmlands ( farmers complained their fields were running red with the blood of Jews, so local police threw white lime powder over the dead bodies)
3. Killing Field Three: Soccer field ( remains found during restoration)
4. Killing Field Four: Orphanage ( children "transfused" blood for wounded)
5. Killing Field Five: The old small craft Airfield

By the end of 1942, Dubno was one of over 3,000 Jewish communities destroyed by the Nazis and their collaborators in the former Russian Territories. Yiskor memorial books, like the one I discovered for Dubno, exist at Yad Vashem, Jerusalem, Israel, and The United States Holocaust Memorial Museum, in Washington, DC. The book *Where Once We Walked* identifies 23,000 Shtetls that existed throughout Europe and the Russian territories before the Holocaust. I was especially moved when I located Dubno in the Valley of Monuments in the lower outdoor area at Yad Vashem. I felt like the Indiana Jones of the Bittelman Family, walking through archeological memorials.

Bella Bittelman met and married Max Needle on Avenue C in New York City in the early 1900's. They produced three sons, Jerry, Harold, and Irwin. My father Harold married Rose Cohen and that is the reason I exist. My sister Susanne and her husband Behic and I have three sons Adam, Ross, and Kraig. There are generations of Bittelman-Needle cousins still being discovered thanks to genealogical and DNA detective work.

If not for the intelligence, courage, love, and actions leading to the survival of at least one family member, from 1935 to 1942, the families mentioned in this book would have been lost. Thank you Grandma Bella for your Intelligence, Courage, and Love. A sheynem dank Bubbe, Liebn, Sheryl.

## Chapter Two

# The Shtetls of Belorussia

The villages of Lyakhovichi, Baranovichi, and Pruzhana are now located in Belarus. For centuries these Jewish, Polish, Lithuanian, Russian multi-ethnic little towns were under Russian and Polish jurisdiction. Like many shtetls east of Europe, organized government persecution, known as pogroms were common to daily life. Sometimes harsh taxes were imposed by the Russians. Other times relocations were ordered by the Polish governments. Violence and imprisonment was sporadic, depending on the affront to often redesigned government laws. Dramatically these policies changed with the invasion of the Nazi German Army's elite mobile squads known as Einsatzgruppen. The violation by the German government of the 1939 Molotov Treaty and their subsequent Operation Barbarossa invasion into the Russia territories brought the treatment of Jews to an unimagined new level.

Belorussian Jews from the shtetl of Lyakhovichi (Lachowicze), my Needle family homeland, were being shot in the villages, the forests, and they also were being deported to concentration camps. My grandfather Max Needle came to America as a boy during the Russian pogroms. The murder of many of the remaining Needle relatives and neighbors is still being discovered. Some Jews in Lyakhovichi survived because they were sent to Siberia by Stalin's secret police for political actions. Moshe Inditzky, a survivor reports that on October 29, 1941, 4000 Jews were undressed and shot into ditches by Nazis and their local collaborators. Chlorine was poured on the bodies, some still moving, between each round of fallen innocent victims. The next day an additional 1500 Jews were placed into ghetto labor camps, until July 20, 1942 when it was determined they were no longer useful and the camp was liquidated. A few hundred were able to flee into the forests and survive with the partisans; others fought with the Red Army against Germany, as did a wounded young Moshe. Research at the Holocaust Center at Yad Vashem in

*Israel Needle family portrait author's grandpa Max front right. Courtesy of snc.*

Israel continues to discover unmarked graves of victims shot by Einsatzgruppen and locals predominantly from 1941–1942.

In 2006 I visited my paternal family village of Lyakhovichi. A small memorial garden is the only evidence that Jews once lived in this village. Head and footstones that once marked Jewish graves were used to support the weight of the German tanks to prevent the wheels from sinking into the mud. A Ukrainian cemetery now is on the site of a former Jewish cemetery. Roads transverse over Jewish bodies long since plowed under the dirt. The woods outside the former shtetl silently hide where Jews once gathered to escape the Lyakhovichi ghetto concentration camp. Tuvia, Asa, & Zus Bielski, Dr.Ezekiel Atlas, and other brave Jewish resistance fighters from this area in Belorussia, were able to save approximately 1200 men, women, and children. Unfortunately, over 10,000 others were slaughtered by 1943, in the ghettos, the forests, and transported to Auschwitz and other Nazi extermination camps.

The following stories of families from the Belarusian shtetls of Pruzhana, Lyakhovichi, and Baranovichi illuminate the tragic destruction or the Shoah, of vibrant Jewish communities in Europe and Soviet Russia.

Pruzhana is in the Brest Oblast and Volhynia regions of Belarus. "White Russia" or "Bela-Rus" was defined by the topography and climate of the area. Harsh snowy winters with small independent shtetls typified Belarussia. Yiddish, Russian, Hebrew, Polish, Ukrainian, and Lithuanian were common languages spoken over the many centuries of exchanging monarchies.

In the 15th century, Pruzhany was under Lithuanian control and occupied by Prussian tribes. In 1588, Poland ruled the area and declared Jews could live in Pruzhana with full rights. An active agricultural community grew. Czarist Russia conquered the city in 1796, with harsh restrictions and pogroms. However, not to be tolerated by Pruzans, an anti-Russification campaign, or socialist Belorussian rebellion occurred in 1880, restoring rights to approximately 2600 Jews. Agriculture, hops and grains, vinegar, alcohol, innkeeping, and guilds developed.

In 1914, Germany and Russia used Belarus as stomping grounds for WWI. Minsk became an important city for world conferences, as Germany, Poland, and Russia all tried to claim the country. The 1921 Treaty of Riga, divided Belarus in half, with the western front going to a predominantly Catholic Poland, and the East to the Orthodox Soviet Union. By then, 4200 Jews settled into the area and became politically active as delegates in the local governments. Jewish owned factories and banks were established, which during the depression later became a reason for antisemitic tension.

In Eastern Europe and Belarus, under Russian rule, Intelligentsia, writers, and teachers of all religions, were outspoken challengers to the local governments from 1930-1937. Jewish intellectuals assimilated into the culture and society throughout Europe and the former Russian territories. They held government political offices and were important in the economic development of these countries. A secular trend developed in the Jewish communities as organizations formed such as the Yevsektsiya, or Jewish communists, Zionists, and the socialist Bund labor movement.

On the western front of Europe and Belorussia, under Polish rule (Riga Treaty), government restrictions were harsh. Polish only was the official state language. Churches and schools were subject to closure if classes were not taught in Polish. Belarusians lost their seats in parliament. The census indicates 375,000 Jews living and working as artists, craftsman, merchants, teachers, doctors, lawyers, and scientists.

Then in 1933, the perfect storm happened. Politically differing ideologies, economic worldwide depression, rising antisemitism, and the humiliating defeat of Germany in WW I, lead to the defeat of democracy by fascism and the election of the Nazi party's charismatic leader Adolph Hitler. By 1939, Russia reclaimed Belarus as Germany occupied Poland.

On June 27, 1941, the German troops occupied Pruzhana. Jewish families were herded into ghetto camps. Sometimes as many as 20 people lived in one of only 60 buildings. The ghetto swelled to approximately 12,000. The increasing numbers were a result of fleeing Jews captured as they entered Belarus, and of local collaborators identifying their Jewish neighbors for a financial bounty. A judenrat, or Jewish council was established within the ghetto to maintain a semblance of order & dignified daily living, education, sanitary systems, and for the distribution of food and medical treatment. Some Jews escaped into the forests. Partisans attempted to free as many Jews as possible, but many refused to leave, believing this would end soon, and the Germans would move on or be defeated by the Russians. Especially among the older victims, weakened health, limited geographic knowledge, love of homeland, and denial of the final horror, prevented their escape. Shootings, transports to Auschwitz, and finally by 1943, within only four days, the ghetto and labor camps in Pruzhana were totally liquidated. After the war, only 12 families returned to find mass ditches with bodies, ancestral graves desecrated, roads built over cemeteries, and the synagogue converted into a power plant. The approximately 60 *Pruzhany* Holocaust survivors lived in a displaced persons camp in Europe before relocating to the United States, Latin America, and Israel.

In Baranowicze, including the surrounding shtetls of Lyakhovichi and Pruzhana, there were three main "Aktions" from March, 1941 to December, 1943. Keeping with German cruelty and irony, they often occurred during Jewish festivals and holidays. Heinrich Himmler created Einsatzgruppen A, B, C, D comprised of roving Nazi units of approximately 600-1,000 men. Their missions were to infiltrate local governments and commission local police to assist in the elimination of Jews from their towns. Recovered German records document the efficiency of machine gun-firing Einsatzgruppen, and local Polish, Lithuanian, Ukrainian, and Latvian police in facilitating this process. *At first it was sickening, but then it's a job, you get used to it*, said one captured collaborator. Although some Belarusians did hide and feed their Jewish friends, too many more were bystanders and worse, collaborators. Jewish victims did attempt to fight back, some through sabotage, others with direct violent confrontations. The main resistance to this insane Shoah, was to remain alive as long as possible.

In Nowogrodek, Belarus on December 1941, members of the Bielski family were murdered by Einsatgruppe B. The surviving Bielski brothers escaped into the woods, returning to avenge their parents and siblings deaths, as seen in the powerful book based movie *Defiance*. Other Jews were also fleeing into the forests, and suddenly ordinary people are asked to do extraordinary things to survive. As a result of the courage of the Bielski Partisans, over 1200 Jews were saved. Tragically approximately 17,000 Jews were murdered in the Lyakhovichi, Baranavichi, & Pruzhana shtetls. Rail lines existed from Belarus to Minsk, Moscow, Warsaw, then in 1942 the Auschwitz-Birkenau hub was built by slave labor POWs and Jews, allowing for the transport and killing of 9,000 more innocent victims.

The following story of the Gershgorn family from Pruzana, Belarussia chronicles a similar shtetl life of hardship, and new lives in Cuba and America. The deportation and internment of Izaak Gershgorn and friend Ben Garberman reveals a dramatic previously unknown tragedy recently revealed to a surviving granddaughter.

Rachel Liba Guralnik and Izak Machman Gershgorn married in Pruzhana and had three girls and six boys. Four died of childhood injuries and illness. Yosef, the first born son, daughter Rosa, and brothers Morris, Isaac, Benjamin, and David remained in Pruzhana with their mother after their father died in 1914 from a work injury. At age 16, in 1921, son Morris left Pruzhana and immigrated to Argentina. He was later able to obtain a visa to America with the promise of marrying an American cousin in Philadelphia. His brother David also emigrated when he turned sixteen but he chose to go to Cuba in 1923, as the quota had been reached for entry into the United States. Morris attempted to get his brother to marry one of their second cousins so he too could come to America, but David refused because he felt he was too young to marry and was making his way and gaining acceptance in Cuba. The brothers became further isolated from each other and communication between them ceased completely from 1926 to 1944. The brothers independently sent money back home to their mother and siblings in Belarus.

David Gershgorn studied Spanish and English adding to the six languages that he already spoke. He worked hard, getting various jobs, such as working in a sugarcane field, electrical trades, jeweler's assistant, stock boy and then salesman at a clothing company. Later while selling samples and traveling to different towns, he was made an offer to buy a small store in San Jose and passionately named it The Truth, "La Verdad." At the young age of 21, while recovering in Havana from surgery, he decided to buy a larger store and move there. It was while in Havana that David was offered the sales territory for the Bristol-Myers company. The move to Havana was fortuitous as he met his future wife, Regina at a dance. It appears to have been love at first sight, as they married in 1936, producing three children, Michael, Raquel, and Stephen.

After Hitler's rise to power in 1933, David sent money back to Pruzana and was able to get his sister to Uruguay, where she married and raised a family until they moved to Israel. David Gershgorn's attempts to communicate with his remaining siblings and mother back in Pruzhana after the 1939 blitzkrieg of Poland by Germany became impossible. The Pruzhana shtetl swelled from 4500 to 12,000 Jews as they fled east from Poland into Belarus. The Germans began to build the ghetto camps to isolate the Jews. The remaining Gershgorn family comprised of Yosef, his wife, three daughters and two sons, Isaac his wife, two sons and two daughters, and their mother Rachelle were moved into the Pruzhana ghetto camp in June 1941. Their friends, the Garberman family, which included Sam and his son Ben, already lived in the area of the camp. But now their neighborhood was a fortified, barbed wire and ten foot high wood fenced in concentration camp.

Sam Garberman did shoe repairs in the ghetto. Ben Garberman, at age 17 was a skilled cabinet maker. Yosef Gershgorn was a blacksmith and Isaac was a textile machinery worker. These young men had useful professions needed by the Nazis. So while others were being shot in the streets, or transported to death camps, Ben, Yosef, and Isaac were released from the ten foot wired, wood fenced ghetto camp daily for forced labor. Then in 1943, they observed Jews being transported to cattle cars at the train station. The train connected to the Baranowicze line, which now connected to Auschwitz-Birkenau. The Pruzhany ghetto camp was being liquidated, some taken to ditches and shot, other to the train cattle cars. One man from each family now remained alive, Yosef and Ben.

The train from Pruzhany via Baranovichi pulled into Auschwitz-Birkenau. There was an immediate selection process, weaker men, women, and children were immediately separated and were sent directly to the gas chambers. Yosef Gershgorn and Ben Garberman survived the selections assigned to harsh labor details. In January 1945, the Germans were given orders from Berlin to evacuate Auschwitz and destroy remaining evidence of death camps. Crematories at Birkenau were bombed, not by the allies, but by the Germans. In the harsh Polish winter, the Jewish surviving victims, with little clothing and sometimes no shoes, were marched through the snow by Nazi guards from camp to camp. Many died in the march from starvation and illness. If you fell into the snow you were immediately shot. Others picked up the shoes of the fallen for warmth. Yosef Gershgorn marched as far as his body would allow him, then was shot as he fell onto the snow frozen ground.

Ben Garberman vowed to stay alive to tell the stories of the victims, and continued on the death march to the Mauthausen concentration camp in Austria. The barely still alive victims were then marched to the Ebensee death camp. On May 6, 1945, the American Armed forces liberated the camp. Ben was then sent to a camp in the Bavarian village of Feldafing. Ironically, this was a former Hitler Youth Camp. It then became a model Displaced Persons Camp, with schools and hospitals for Holocaust survivors.

After regaining his health, Ben applied for a visa to join relatives in the United States. An aunt living in Pennsylvania was able to sponsor him and a visa to the United States was issued. Ben was told that others from his shtetls were also living in Pennsylvania, and he made arrangements to meet with Morris Gershgorn, now Morris Gordon, to inform him of the fate of his family.

Around this same time, in Havana, near David Gershgorn's store was Hotel Nacional, frequented by visiting American tourists and locals. One day David was approached by a woman who thought he was Morris Gershgorn from Pennsylvania. He told her that he was David Gershgorn, but that he did have a brother Morris living America, who he had not seen since 1921. The woman took a picture of David and upon return to Philadelphia shared it with Morris. Morris flew to Cuba and convinced his brother to begin the immigration process of getting David and Rifka and both families' visas to the United States.

Ben Garberman is 85 years old and now lives in New Jersey, ironically minutes away from Michael, son of the late David and Rifka Gershgorn. Their daughter Raquel Gordon named after her grandmother Rachel who died in Auschwitz-Birkenau, lives in Florida and is the mother of Salise, Joe, and Adam and adoring grandmother of Aiden and Ella. Raquel has remarried and with her husband they have a total of seven children and nine grandchildren.

## Chapter Three

# A Baby Girl, a German Displaced Persons Camp, and the Hope of a Nation

Berlin, 1947: the birth of a baby girl. How can the birth of this one infant restore Jewish hope? Displaced Persons Camps were established by the allies in Europe at the conclusion of the Second World War. Allied and Nazi army barracks and even former concentration camps, were used as DP camps. The purpose was to provide temporary housing to survivors of Hitler's horrible Nazi concentration-extermination-death camps. The emphasis should have been on the word temporary, but as was soon discovered, many survivors remained in DP camps for years, as they had no place to go. Many families were totally destroyed, thereby leaving surviving children orphaned. Jewish adult survivors still faced antisemitism when they attempted to return to their towns, often threatened by their neighbors with continued genocide. Patriation was therefore very difficult. Attempts to emigrate to the Mideast and to the United States were met with government quotas limiting Jewish movement overseas. With the help of Eleanor Roosevelt after her husband, FDR's death and during Truman's presidency, quotas of Jews to America finally were expanded. In the Mideast, freedom fighters overcame British blockades, gained world support, and with the creation of the state of Israel in 1948, European Jewish Holocaust survivors now could establish new lives as Israeli citizens.

Word very slowly reached the outside world as to the magnitude of destruction of the Jewish communities in Europe and Russia. It took many years for people to be able to leave the DP camps to be united with relatives who often were strangers and known in name only. During this painful waiting period, Jewish communities were established within the Displaced Persons camps. The most remarkable testament to the strength of these new communities was the desire to restore Jewish pride. The hope of the Jewish Nation rested in the defining of what it meant to be a Jew, and a human being, versus a Holocaust survivor. Intelligence, courage, and survival was not just based on surviving Nazi extermination attempts in camps and villages, but the continuance of the Jewish Nation as defined by Jews alone!

Schools were established to continue the much valued academic and religious teaching of children. People were given jobs both inside the DP camps, as well as in the towns nearby. Curfews were mandated to keep track of the DP residents. It became apparent that social connections were important in the post-Holocaust healing process. Those that had no one needed someone. People began to feel again, having shut off emotions in order to survive and cope with the daily horrors of Hitler's Holocaust. Singing, dancing, celebrating life where there had only been death for so long, now felt overwhelmingly good.

What could possibly be the ultimate revenge of Hitler's Nazi Holocaust? The answer was clear to those in DP camps: the continuance of the Jewish Nation, no matter where Jews live. Young men and women began to establish new families. These were the adult children, whose entire families were murdered, now forming new unions. Wedding dresses made from army parachute silks were in vogue. The entire DP camp became a shtetl, a village, a celebrating community as it was in Eastern Europe and the Russian territories. Not too surprising, how sweet the revenge, when a year after these marriages, a brand new Jewish baby would be born. This is the story of Gitel Benczman, a beautiful blond baby girl born in a Displaced Persons camp in Germany to Holocaust survivors Julia Pruzen and Chino Benczman.

The town of Niemenczyn, like many in the Vilnius region, was ruled by Russian, Polish, and now Lithuanian governments. Before WWII, thirty-five percent of the population was Jewish in this beautiful Polish resort village. With pine forests lining the area for miles and gala lakes dotting the landscape in the Southeast, Niemenczyn was the ideal resort town. Children would enjoy long days of playing barefoot in the streets and adults would take each moment a second at a time. No one rushed in Niemenczyn, it was the twenties, no one needed to rush. Each summer visitors would flock to this getaway town to experience the calm and serenity that Niemenczyn had to offer. After the summer, they would return back to their hometowns, but for some, like the Pruzens, Niemenczyn was home.

The Pruzens lived along the Wilja River in a large house, suitable for a family of eighteen. Together, they ran a grocery store and lived a simple life. Schlome, one of the eighteen, was known to be the most handsome of the sons; this was nearly inarguable with the numerous women that would surround him. Eventually the time came to settle down and have a family. An arranged marriage to Sarah resulted in the births of Julia, Chaja, and Mulik.

Julia Pruzen was carefree, intelligent, and an ambitious young girl. She felt great joy from the simple things in life as she would often lose herself in books and the natural beauty of Niemenczyn. Julia was eager to attend school and greatly wished to attend the university to study banking. She pushed aside the thread and thimble homemaker role at age 15, for a summer job in banking in Warsaw.

As in many shtetls Thursday was market day in Niemenczyn. The marketplace, or in Yiddish yarid, was the axis of community life where townspeople would buy, sell, and barter commodities from sugar to fish to flowers to dishes. It was a lively and joyous punctuation to the week with the exception of the very last market day in Niemenczyn. On September 20th, 1941, the Nazis had the village of Niemenczyn on their list for *purification*. They demolished Niemenczyn in effort to rid the town of its second class citizens. The image of the beautiful resort town and its spirit would never be the same. Many townspeople initially thought that the Nazi roundup was to enslave Jews for forced labor during the German occupation. The raid was loud, brutal, and swift. After 400 shootings in the street, the Nazi plan of Jewish extermination became undeniably clear.

Julia and Chaja were about twelve kilometers east of Niemenczyn working on a farm. The farmer told them of the Nazi violence in their shtetl, and advised them to run further east away from the massacre. Many in the Pruzen families were trapped in the Niemenczyn massacre. This included their aunts, uncles, cousins, and their mother Sarah and five year old brother Mulik.

The sisters ended up in the nearby town of Kiemieliszki. The Nazi Einsatzgruppen mobile troops were raiding the countryside town by town, and Kiemieliszki had not yet met the fate of Niemenczyn. The next day they were surprised by the arrival of their father Schlome's brother Mickel. Uncle Mike was a Corporal in the Polish Army, returning back to Niemenczyn to warn his family of the approaching Germans. While traveling through the dense forest he heard the far off pandemonium of machine guns and cries followed by utter silence. He helplessly knew he could do nothing to save them.

Mike told his nieces to travel with him to Postawy, on the Lithuanian-Belarusian Lake border to stay with relatives. Julia and Chaja stayed with their paternal Aunt Beila and her husband Mendl in Postawy. It became dangerous for so many to be clustered in one house, so Chaja and Uncle Mike went to a nearby friend's house. Mike learned that his brother Chonon survived the massacre and was also on the run, setting out to find him. He promised his young nieces that he would return. He knew that they were not only his responsibility, but members of what was left of his once large family.

As a Polish army sharp shooter and Corporal, Mike was able to sneak into the Vilna Ghetto. He bravely risked his life to help hide fellow escaping Jews. Some righteous gentiles hid Jews, others realized the possible profit, as there was a Nazi bounty for each turned in Jew. Mike, as a skilled electrician was able to barter with rescuers, doing repairs in return for safe hidings. He took responsibility for each Jew he hid, checking back on them as he could.

There were two main forms of assisted hiding during the Holocaust. One form of hiding was in which the refugees literally went into hidden spaces. Another form was hiding in plain sight, assuming Christian family member roles in the safe homes in which they were hidden. Like many other hidden Jews during the Holocaust, the Pruzen girls were transplanted from home to home and experienced both types several times. One time Julia was in hiding with a shoemaker and his family. Because of his profession, the location was busy with clients. Julia would hide cramped between the oven and the wall unable to move, without food or water for many hours.

Chaja and Julia missed each other as they separately hid to survive. They changed safe homes often as the Nazis got closer. They longed for their Uncle Mike's weekly visits. He was their only link to family and he would update each of the girls on the status of the war and how the other sister was doing. It gave Julia great relief to hear that her little sister was safe in hiding, or at least that was what she believed. No Jew was ever truly safe, nor were the families that sheltered them.

The last home Julia hid in was that of a good Christian family. She was not in good health at the time and the Polish family risked their lives to hide her in a rustic barn. On Christmas Eve the family let Julia into their home, and dressed her in holiday clothes, complete with fancy rouge for her pale cheeks. Suddenly there was a loud knock on the door. No one expected that the Nazis would perform a random check on a Christian holiday. The family had no choice but to let the Nazis in to avoid suspicion. They greeted the soldiers and entertained them with food and wine. Julia although petrified with fear, had to protect herself and the host family. The air was tense as Julia noticed that one of the soldiers was starring at her. The soldier demanded all but Julia to leave the room. Her mind and heart raced, worrying that he did not believe that she was a visitor to the farm family even though red haired Julia did not appear Jewish. Julia had been able to hide in plain sight, acting the role of a non-Jewish character in a play.

While the German soldier paced the room, Julia thought of the horrific possibilities. Was he going to rape her? Was he planning to kill her? Would he kill the family who risked all to hide her? Julia must have been the best actress as she and the soldier locked eyes. Without explanation, he ordered the troops to leave. Julia survived another day, but her relief was short lived. The host family apologized, but told her she must leave immediately. She had become a liability to them all. Julia was again on the run, forced back into the forest.

Julia lost contact with her sister Chaja and Uncle Mike. She especially hoped her sister was safe. Mike had contacted a farmer who was a distant relative to provide shelter for Chaja. The farmer liked her charming personality. Chaja and the farmer's son were the same age and fell in love. Unaware to all, the farmer was mentally unstable. In a fit of jealous rage he brutally attacked Chaja and shot his son, tragically killing them both.

Meanwhile in the forest, Julia promised to fight to remain alive. She followed the campfires to the underground Jewish partisan fighters. She wanted to join and fight with them. Although fueled by ambition and anger, these strong emotions were no match for the physical deterioration she suffered in the freezing forest. She was only 90 pounds when rescued by the partisans.

When Julia finally exited the forest, she was unaware that the war had ended. Victorious allied forces placed her in Schlactensee, a displaced person's camp in West Berlin. Even though Julia was fragile, she was lucky to be alive and she had personally triumphed. The adjustment to placement in a displaced persons camp was very difficult. The world would never again be normal. It was here that she learned from Uncle Mike the horrible fate of her beloved sister Chaja. Julia was one of approximately 250,000 Jews to survive the Holocaust and enter displaced persons camps in Europe. The allied commands, the United Nations Relief and Rehabilitation Administration, and Jewish refugee organizations attempted to find families and friends who may have survived, as well as family members in other countries. These camps became more than a place to recover and find survivors; they resembled the soul of Jewish shtetls prior to the Holocaust. Displaced persons camps provided refugees with a sense of community. Here, each individual was dependent on the strength, determination and optimism of the other.

The displaced persons camp provided critical medical care and fellowship with other survivors necessary to bring Julia back to health. As months went by, Julia regained her outgoing spirit. She loved the nightlife in West Berlin and her aura attracted everyone around her. It was her radiance that attracted Chino Benczman a handsome, charming man twelve years older. Chino was from Rovno, a Polish-Russian province. As a young boy he enjoyed traveling theater and Russian folk songs. Chino spent the Holocaust in a harsh Siberian work camp after being captured by the Russians as a Polish soldier. He was handsome and personable and loved life like Julia. His suave style got him far in the DP camp, buying and selling what he could in the black market from chocolates to nylons.

It was not long before Julia and Chino fell in love. Their wedding in the DP camp was simple. Julia's girlfriend provided her with a dress and Chino bought a suit and ring with his black market funds. The DP Jewish family celebrated their union signifying a continuance of Jewish life.

Not too long after their wedding the couple experienced a miracle of love and life. They were blessed with a beautiful baby girl who they named Gitel, after Chino's murdered mother. Childbirth was not easy for Julia, although she had regained strength with the help of those in the displaced person's camp, she was still relatively weak. Due to excessive bleeding, mother and newborn almost died during a difficult labor. But once again, Julia survived. Chino was able to hire a nanny to take care of baby Gitel as Julia recovered. The nanny continued in their employ, but seemed to be getting too attached to Gitel, who had beautiful blond hair and was as a toddler speaking fluent German. Julia fearing the nanny might kidnap Gitel, fired her and cared for her child herself.

Julia and Chino decided to immigrate to Israel. They felt the family would be safe there. They could not return to their family homes, as they had been confiscated by locals refusing to return them to Jews. Antisemitism still existed in Poland and damage in the towns was extensive. Unfortunately for the small family, they had no required sponsors in Israel. Uncle Mike immigrated to Canada, changing his name to Michael Levitan. Then through Jewish agencies like HIAS, the Hebrew Immigrant Aid Society, a sponsor was found in America. Julia's paternal Uncle Sol was found to be living in New Orleans, Louisiana. But it took years for the family to finally obtain visas to leave

*Chino, Gitel, Julia Benczman in a Displaced Persons camp Berlin, Germany, 1946. Courtesy of Gale Benczman Sussman.*

West Berlin. Finally in 1953, Uncle Sol sponsored his niece, her husband, and five year old Gitel. Although the family was grateful to be in the United States, Julia was not happy in New Orleans. The family learned of a Jewish community of survivors living in Milwaukee, Wisconsin and relocated there.

The Benczmans opened a convenience store. They were determined to succeed in life, considering what they endured. Julia and Chino's top priority was Gitel; it was important to them to provide her with the best that they could and to protect her. Gitel attended a special English language immersion program for immigrant children of Holocaust survivors. The innovative program was sponsored by Jewish welfare agencies designed to prepare young children for entry into American public school. Through songs and games, Gitel had fun and quickly learned English. Their teacher, Mrs. Dorethea Pinko often thought about the immigrant children and their families. She decided to search for the children and 50 years later Gale (Gitel) and her teacher had an emotional reunion in Florida.

Young Gitel Benczman was basically raised in her parent's convenience store. It was a partial playground, with free treats, and a family obligation. Gitel often found herself as the family translator of written and spoken English for her parents. Her mother cautioned Gitel to keep her religion private, a lingering post traumatic Holocaust fear.

Julia and Chino kept Holocaust talk to a minimal in their home. They did not believe it would help Gitel to discuss their stories. Although their pain was unspoken, it was so intense that words were often not needed to feel their sorrow. There were other survivors in their neighborhood; after all that is why they moved to Milwaukee. Gitel learned of Esther, her kind, elderly neighbor's Holocaust trauma, when she asked about the tattooed numbers on her arm. Esther had been a victim of sterilization experiments in Auschwitz. Since she could not have children of her own she enjoyed Gitel's visits to her apartment.

Taking two buses and wearing bargain clothing, Gitel traveled to a school in a better neighborhood for her secondary education. Her parents had instilled in her the importance of education. After Gitel graduated she planned to continue helping her parents in the grocery store, which she knew was their pride and symbol of their survival. Julia would not tolerate this standard for her only child. She pushed Gitel to attend college, once again emphasizing the importance of higher education. As Gitel struggled in her freshman studies, Julia would constantly reiterate that it was important to never give up. The college student struggled with the guilt of complaining about small things in comparison to her parents' life as courageous survivors. She needed to bring pride to the family and achieve what they did not have the opportunity to experience due to the Shoah.

Gitel decided it was time to choose Gale as her Americanized name. Gale was grateful for her mother's encouragement. She obtained her Bachelors degree in Education, studying to be a History teacher. Gale Benczman continued her education obtaining a Masters Degree in Counseling. While doing an internship, she met Stuart Sussman a parole officer at the state prison. It was not long before Gale was heading a household of her own, continuing the Pruzen-Benczman lineage.

During this time, Julia and Chino continued to work hard in their grocery store. They were grateful for their life in America and wanted to help others. The store was located in a poor neighborhood and they often gave the children extra food. Julia even paid for the wedding of one of their female employees. Chino hired a fellow survivor in need to help in the store. Sadly, a short time later their helper was fatally shot in a hate crime. The horror that Julia and Chino experienced thirty years prior came rushing back. This post traumatic stress caused Chino to subsequently suffer a heart attack. Exorbitant medical bills caused them to lose the store. Gale became stronger, now able to help her parents. She finally understood the relationship of being an adult child of survivors. She also knew the importance of creating a third generation, post Holocaust. Gale and Stuart produced two daughters, Heather and Stacy, while she continued her work at a women's assertiveness group. A great success for Gale, and a proud homage to her parents, was her creation of the Second Generation Organization for adult children of Holocaust survivors in 1981in Milwaukee, with the support of her good friend Sandy Hoffman. This organization continues today with nationwide chapters and several spin-off organizations, now including Third Generation grandchildren of survivors.

In 1986, Gale relocated her entire family for a job opportunity in Florida. Ahead of her time, she would work in the field of obesity health in wellness. Since Julia and Chino no longer had the store, they welcomed helping raise their granddaughters. As Chino aged and his heart weakened, he chose to rediscover Judaism as spiritual comfort for depression and latent anxieties. Recent research indicates that some Holocaust survivors have developed late onset Post Traumatic Stress Disorder (PTSD.) Professionals may have misdiagnosed survivor symptoms as Alzheimer's, and age related depression, versus late onset Holocaust PTSD, especially as they aged closer to death. Contently, Chino and Julia lived their remaining years close to Gale and her family until their deaths at age 82 and 73, respectively.

Throughout her life, Gale was constantly aware of her role and obligation as a member of the Second Generation. This probably was the reason Gale dedicated her life to counseling others. Like her parents, she too became a strong survivor, when she defeated kidney cancer. If not overcoming enough trauma, she and her husband lost their home during Hurricane Charlie. Stuart has also overcome experimental surgery for heart disease. Through all this, Gale continues to raise funds for cancer research and other charities in Central Florida.

Julia Pruzen and Chino Benczman left a legacy of strength, perseverance, ambition, and love of life. Gale and Stuart share this spirit with their adult children Heather and Stacy, named after Schlome, and grandchildren Emily and Dylan. As a hobby, Gale sings and dances in a local performers club. She clearly has inherited the vivacious spirit and talents of her parents. The pride in Jewish identity and the sorrow of Shoah is remembered annually by Gale. Due to the intelligence, courage, and survival of Julia and Chino, Gale Benczmen Sussman and her offspring are the living legacies signifying the triumph over the Holocaust.

*Chapter Four*

# A Second Generation Perspective, Trauma, and Success

I believe the damage done to families of the Holocaust, did not end with their murders, or even with their survival. The damage to subsequent generations becomes a slow insipid awareness. Sometimes it will be a baby naming or a marriage that triggers their pain. A movie, news article, discovered photograph, or a document hidden in a forgotten box, can cause inquisitiveness, but at the same time anxiety. Second Generations birthing and raising of their own children raises question of odd behaviors of their survivor parents. A dear friend and Second Generation adult child of two survivors shares her story.

## A SECOND GENERATION SPEAKS

At this writing I am a 58 year old woman, having had both parents die young. I believe their deaths are related to their concentration camp internment. When I visit doctors and they ask questions on their medical forms about my parents' health history, how should I answer them? How would I ever know which illnesses were genetic versus the trauma of the camps?

I found out at a very young age what a concentration camp was. My earliest memories are when my younger sister Phyllis and I were sitting on the living room floor watching TV with my parents. We were watching a show about WWII. The narrator was talking about the concentration camps in Nazi Germany. My parents just sat there listening and then I heard my mother say "They are not showing and telling like it really was during the Holocaust." My mouth and eyes widened. Now the questions started to pour out of my mouth. Mom, I said, "How do you know"? My mother said "because I was there." My father rarely ever spoke about the holocaust or about his family. All he ever said was that he was the only son of 8 children who survived the

27

ordeals. I found out just recently that he was a grave digger in Auschwitz. My mother who did speak of the camps was at Bergen Belsen. Both of them were taken during their teenage years.

My parents spoke with an accent and told me that they came from Poland and how they had to learn English and take a test to become American citizens. But this new information about concentration camps was a complete shock. There, right on the TV it showed the most horrific resemblance of human beings that I had ever seen. My parents sat emotionless. Inexplicably I felt guilty that I wasn't there to protect them. I was afraid to upset them for fear it would be another form of punishment. Suddenly, they became fragile in my eyes, needing my protection.

My parents never let me sleep over friends' houses. It was only when doing an interview for this book that I discovered their reasons. They feared I would not return home; taken in the night, or on the way home from school, as happened to many Jewish children. Because they never expressed their reasons, it was difficult for me to understand this. I was so angry at them for depriving me of this childhood experience. I held the anger in for 46 years!

I also didn't understand why my friends got to visit with their grandparents and I couldn't. For that matter I had very few relatives at all. My mother had one brother in Canada who survived, but that was so far to go for a hug on a Sunday drive. Again, my parents never offered an explanation, until the wall of silence came crashing down the night we watched that Holocaust movie. I then felt responsible for them and had to protect them from harm. I took over their survivor guilt.

When I became older, I searched for support and became a member of "Second Generation." This organization is for of children of holocaust parents. I thought by joining this group I would be able to understand my parents better. I could never understand why my parents would never say "I love you." Was it a fear of having something taken away again? The only time my mother told me she loved me was when she was dying. She also gave me her final advice "be careful of the Germans!" Can you imagine having those thoughts until the day you die?

Being a parent now it is very important for me to show love to my children. I also tell them about their grandparents' horrific experiences in the concentration camps. I believe my parents felt a duty to have children in order to continue the Jewish community; otherwise the Nazis would have won!

—Shirley Silberstein Schuman, Spring 2009

Shirley's father, Herman Silberstein was born in 1928, one of eight children and the only son in his family. He came from the Siedlce shtetl outside of

Warsaw, Poland. Like many little towns in eastern Poland, it was under the governance of Czarist Russia for a period of time, and then returned to its Polish origins. Jews inhabited the town since the 16th century. Innkeepers, due to the growth of hops and grains in the area, merchants, artists, and later medical and educational professionals flourished as pre-WWII occupations. Intermittent periods of antisemitism and pogroms (government targeted violence & restrictions) against the Jews were common throughout the history of the region, but Jews remained in their shtetls. Warsaw was only 90 kilometers to the west of Siedlce, so the Jewish communities shared an itinerant Rabbi. By 1900, approximately forty percent of the 24,000 Siedclian population was Jewish, or about 10,000 Jews. As Jews began to assimilate into the culture, secular organizations formed, like the Bund, similar to modern labor unions. Political movements such as the Polish Socialist Party and Zionism were popular among young secular Jews. Antisemitism was common among Catholic Poles, and Herman had his nose broken a few times by local school boys. Jews often were caught between the German, Polish and Red Russian army occupations in the early twentieth century, but it was not until March 1941,

*Miriam Silberstein, Siedlce, Poland, photo hidden in Auschwitz by brother Herman. Courtesy of Shirley Silberstein Schuman.*

with the Nazi occupation did they realize their final fate. The killing of Jewish leaders and intelligentsia, was followed by isolation into ghetto internment camps with limited food and poor sanitary conditions. Then in August 1942 the ghetto concentration camps were emptied, the Siedlce Jews were marched to the train station, and deported to the Treblinka extermination camp. By November 1942, Nazi commanders could report to Himmler that Siedlce was "Juden Frei." Blonde, blue-eyed Herman Silberstein was young, strong, and healthy so during the initial selections, he was needed as a grave digger, thus surviving in Auschwitz. For six years in Auschwitz he was able to conceal one photograph of his sister, with the hope of uniting the eight siblings after the war. Herman and the photograph only survived. He was transported to an allied displaced persons camp after liberation.

Shirley's mother, Gitla Beitner, was born in 1924, the middle of six children, in Strzemieszyce, Poland. It is 52 kilometers west of Krakow. It was historically under Polish rule for most of its existence, but records indicate monarchy control from Prussia, Russia, and Austria also. Clergy from Krakow appear to have had major religious authority over the town. In fact Pope Paul officiated in this region while a priest. A Holocaust survivor reported he received communion wafers from the priest as food in order to stay alive. Industrialization brought rails and mining to the town at the end of the 19th century. The twentieth century population of Strzemieszyce was approximately 7,000 people, of which 2,000 were registered in the census as Jewish. They worked as artisans, small shopkeepers, doctors, teachers, and chemists in the phosphorus factory. Young people attended the nearby high school in Bedzin for higher educations. The Jewish cemetery was located in nearby Slawkow. Suddenly in 1939 Germany invaded Poland and occupied Strzemieszyce on September 5. Jews were shot in the streets and stores were plundered. Jews were forced into labor and had to wear white armbands with the Star of David. Ethnic Germans and local Poles moved into the nicer apartments of Jews and took over their businesses. The Jews were moved into poorer, crowded shared housing with many families. A factory was taken over by the Nazis and Jews were forced into metal working labor. In the winter of 1941, yellow stars replaced the white bands, and warm clothing was confiscated for the Nazis. Some Jews were bused to the factory in Bedzin for labor. In June of 1942, deportations to death camps began of those Jews who were no longer needed by the Nazis, often too weak from starvation and illness to be useful. Nazis were notorious for using false information, "tricks" to "relocate" Jews calmly to their death. On June 15, 1943 all remaining Strzemieszyce Jews were imprisoned and most killed at Auschwitz. Gitla Beitner was one of the lucky Jews, forced into hard labor in the Nazi controlled factories. Her cousin worked in the ghetto kitchens and would smuggle Gitla food to keep her strength up. When the final round up occurred, she was in Bedzin and taken to the Bergen-Belsen concentration camp. Unlike Auschwitz, Belsen did not have gas chambers. The camp was in the northwest city of Bergen, Germany, and the Nazis preferred to have extermination camps further east, away from the German populace. POW's and Jews were shot and hung, and thrown into mass ditches, but not gassed. In March 1945, Anne & Margot Frank died of Typhus, just days before the British troops liberated this camp. Gitla, also suffering from Diphtheria and Typhus survived and was taken to a displaced persons camp in Bergen. This DP camp was a former German military camp, and subsequently renamed the Begen-Belsen Displaced Persons camp.

The Begen-Belsen Displaced Persons camp was run by the allied forces, under British control. Israeli partisans from then Palestine, Eretz Israel, came to the camp to provide education and medical support to survivors. The allies needed good mechanics to repair and maintain vehicles, and after physically recovering, a survivor named Herman was hired. One day another survivor, Simon Beitner introduced Herman to his sister Gitla. The couple married in 1946. They applied to immigrate to America, but like most survivors had no legal documents of identity. The U.S. Consulate accepted affidavits from the

*Certificate of Identity papers 1947 Herman & Gitla Beitner Silberstein. Courtesy of Shirley Silberstein Schuman.*

DP camp commanders, along with physical identifications, in order to establish Certificates of Identity, instead of passports. Sadly and forever, Harry's Auschwitz tattoo number 128326 would be a distinguishing identifier.

The thought of the Silbersteins returning to their homes in Poland were quickly ended when reports of a pogrom came from Kielce, Poland. Kielce is situated midway between Warsaw and Krakow, in southeastern Poland. Forty former Jewish citizens had returned to a group apartment home after the liberation. They were waiting to reclaim their homes in their village. A false accusation led to an antisemitic mob attack with guns and clubs against men, woman, and children. Some innocent Jews were even thrown off a train as it pulled into the station. Local police provided very little protection, some even participating in the assault. The July 1946 massacre led many Polish Jews to realize they could never go home again. Many immigrated to Palestine, Latin America, and the United States. Jewish organizations pled with Pope Pius to condemn this assault, but he refused. In 1947, Herman and Gitla arrived in New York, USA.

Herman and Gitla Silberstein in 1953 became Harry and Gertrude Silberstein when they became United States Citizens. Daughters Shirley and Phyllis were born in Brooklyn, NY. It would be Shirley as the oldest daughter that would experience the intergenerational trauma of the Holocaust. "I felt like it happened to me," she said in one interview. For many years, her parents never spoke of their horrible experiences. It was a secret mystery in order to protect their children, or maybe themselves, or both. So much of their concentration camp experience was not only horrific, but humiliating, degrading, and inhumane. After a family viewing of a Holocaust movie, the psychological flood gates opened with information, often overwhelming Shirley. Harry and Gertrude's need to protect their daughter resulted in incomprehensible restrictions on their teenage daughter. Survivors need to protect their own, and they often have lingering distrust of government and local police authorities. The sisters' feelings, emotional and physical childhood pain may have been invalidated, as "our pain pales in comparison to that which our parents experienced." A need to protect their survivor parents was common. Mistakes in parenting were more often made with Shirley as the first born. This is common in all families, but perhaps more so with second generation children. Survivors lost their own role models as their parents perished in the Holocaust. Anger was a guilt ridden emotion when second generation children wondered why their parents did not fight back. It is only later; after much reading and support group discussions can they understand how the sophisticated, systematic deprivation prevented this.

Shirley indicated that her father never celebrated his birthday; she didn't even know the date until locating his naturalization papers. The concept of survivor guilt should be part of any second generation support group discussion. Finally, issues of trust and distrust of non-Jews should not surprise children of survivors. Even living in the land of the free, Shirley's father was deeply troubled by discrimination and antisemitism in America. Sadly, Harry died at the young age of 47 of a heart aneurism and Gertrude by age 65 of a stroke and cancer.

Shirley and husband Mickey have two daughters, Hallie and Stacy, and a grandchild. This multigenerational existence would not have been possible if not for the intelligence and courage of her survivor parents. Shirley and all Second Generation, and now Third Generation adult children of survivors, are the Maggids (storytellers) of the Shoah.

## POSTSCRIPT

In the spring of 2011, I contacted the International Tracing Service (I.T.S) in Germany to try to find more information about the Holocaust fates of Herman Silberstein and Gitla Beitner. Since the only thing other than them to survive

*International Tracing Service staff & Dr. Cohn, June 21, 2011. Bad Arolsen, Germany, D. Circle photographer. Courtesy of snc.*

*Shirley Schuman & Dr. Cohn reviewing newly discovered Nazi documents of Herman & Gitla Silberstein, July 17, 2011, Florida, M. Schuman photographer. Courtesy of snc.*

the Holocaust was one small photograph, I wanted to try to find some artifacts for my second generation friend Shirley.

On June 21, 2011 the "trace" request proved fruitful. I spent the day with the amazing team at the I.T.S. in Bad Arolsen, Germany. I returned with copies of newly discovered documents of both Shirley's parents. A major surprise was finding Nazi documents listing Herman Zilberstein as an electrician. He was not at just one camp as originally disclosed, but Herman was transferred four times to different camps: Auschwitz, Majdanek-Lubin, Buchenwald, and then in the last days of the war back to Auschwitz. The amount of details in these original documents tracing the horrific six years of both survivors from 1941-1947 was overwhelming.

We sincerely thank the I.T.S. document tracing research members.

*Chapter Five*

# Au Revoir Les Juifs de Paris

France has a long history of anti-Semitism. Although a Jewish community had survived for centuries in central Europe, life for Jews vacillated between expulsion, murder, and acceptance. It was not difficult then when Hitler and fascism replaced democracy in Germany in 1933, for a divided France under the Vichy government to follow suit. Through a well planned and implemented propaganda campaign, the Nazi Socialist Party easily infiltrated French society. Assimilated Jews in both Germany and France now became non-citizens. Judaism became a race instead of a religion. They were now seen as a threat to the economic and political stability of the Europe. Sanctioned laws from the highest levels of government down to the local police institutionalized antisemitism. Expulsion and discrimination now accelerated into violence, deportation, and extermination. Hitler did his homework well and understood the history of French anitsemitism, as it is revealed in the pages to follow. The destruction of the Jewish community, the Shoah, is seen through the eyes of a 6 year old boy, Pierre, and Les Enfants de Paris.

The Roman destruction of the Holy Temple in Jerusalem led fleeing Israelites to Europe. French Jews became well established in commerce, finance, medicine, theater, and literature. They even quickly learned viticulture, growing the finest grapes used ceremonially by the Catholic churches and synagogues on the Sabbath. In southern France and throughout central Europe and Germany, artifacts from the 5th century such as coins, menorahs, and embedded Sabbath wall locks, are indicative of early settlements. A 6th century synagogue was built on the Ile de la Cite, Paris. The 12th century second Crusades brought great hardship on the Jews. Jews were non-human cattle, King Augustus declared, and Christian citizen loans held by Jewish money lenders were made void, property was confiscated, and Jews were expelled from Paris. Jews were allowed to return to Paris in the 13th century,

however they had to wear identification badges. This recurring pattern of expulsion and return throughout the centuries continued as new kings ascended
to the thrones.

In 1349, the Black Plague infected people in regions such as Alsace. As
Jews practiced religiously required health codes, they often were spared death
from the plague. Ignorant accusations of Jews causing the illness resulted in
killings and expulsions. Once again Jews later returned, sometimes hiding
their religion, as in the case of the Marranos, or Spanish and Portugese Jews
in the 16-18 centuries. Immigrants from Eastern Europe, such as Russia and
Poland also entered France through the port of Nice. By the 18th century,
Paris had a vibrant Jewish community. The first Kosher restaurant opened
in 1721, followed by a synagogue. Jewish rights as citizens were established
following the French Revolution. Napoleon, a century later would create a
department of religion within the government, allowing him to levy taxes and
create domestic controls.

By the 19th and early 20th centuries Paris had become a cultural and intel-
lectual hub for Jews and all worldly scholars and artists. A rabbinical semi-
nary still in existence today was opened. Jewish notables appeared in every
aspect of Parisian life, such as Bernhardt, Rothschild, Proust, Hugo, Herzl,
and Chagall. A scandalous set-back occurred for the Jewish community when
one of their own was charged with treason. Captain Alfred Dreyfus in 1894
was charged with treason, accused of being a spy for Germany. Born in Alsace, which was transferred to Germany, he was fluent in German, Yiddish,
and French. Tried and convicted, he was sentenced to life in prison. Ten years
later writer Emile Zola exposed discriminatory evidence withheld by French
government officials. Dreyfus was exonerated, reinstated into the army, later
earning the rank of Lieutenant Colonel. Subsequent Jewish organizations
formed, such as the Federation des Societes Juives de France, to meet the
needs of approximate 300,000 Jews living in France in 1939.

May 1940, Germany occupies France under the pretense of protecting it
from hostile allied forces. The country becomes divided by followers of the
Nazi sympathetic Vichy government, versus the democratic government prior
to the occupation. The insidious Nazi propaganda machine applies the previously successful German Nuremberg Laws to French Jewish citizens. The
result is the rise in state sanctioned antisemitism, restrictions on business,
homes, curfews, Jews in public places, and the required wearing of L'Etoile
de David, the yellow Jewish star badge. From 1941 through 1944 Parisians
witnessed arrests, containment, incarceration in transit camps, such as Drancy
and Gurs and the Vel'D'Hiv event. This all led to the final deportations to
Auschwitz and other death camps and deaths of approximately 100,000
French Jewish citizens.

Many Jews survived by fleeing to North Africa, where France had established colonies. After the war, some stayed in Algeria, Morocco and Tunisia; others were repatriated to France, or immigrated to Israel and the United States. Today, about 300,000 Jews live in Paris, double that number throughout all of France, or approximately four percent of the total population considers itself Jewish. Antisemitism still occurs, often in the form of vandalism and graffiti to cemeteries or synagogues. The French National Museum is actively working to try to return artwork stolen by Nazis to Jewish families. Jewish councils, synagogues, museums, educational institutes, and several significant Holocaust memorials exist in Paris. The French government and Jewish organizations have cooperated in restoring the historical integrity to prior Jewish districts in Paris. But to this day, the events of the summers of 1941 and 1942 remain a national stain due to the actions of the collaborating Vichy government, the collaborating French Police, and too many antisemitic Nazi sympathetic French citizens.

It was August 20, 1941 and people were shopping and going to work as usual in the 11th arrondissement, or district. Paris is divided into districts, each with its own local police headquarters and administrators. Prior to the war, religion did not appear on the French census. Now under German occupation most Jews living in Paris had registered as required and in order to receive food ration coupon books. Theodor Dannecker, the SS captain in charge of the French "Jewish Question" ordered the registered files be color coded by professions, nationality, and street. This made the Aktion, the German campaign, easy to carry out. Jewish citizens were stopped in the streets and asked for their papers. Homes in the district were searched door to door by the 11th precinct police. Under Gestapo orders, the metro stations were closed, blocking possible escape. Buses, ordinary school buses, transported the Jews to Drancy, a transit camp previously built for about 800 prisoners of war. By the following day, the camp now had ten times the number of innocent inmates, whose only crime was being born Jewish. Those returning from school or work found notices on their doors to report the next day to their precincts, which was when many were saved fleeing the country or going into hiding. Lawyers from the Paris Bar Association were among those professionals in this "rafle" or raid. The inmates had no possessions, no toiletries, and lived in crowded unhealthy conditions, resulting in lice and illness. After three months, the gendarmes allowed the Red Cross to deliver some parcels and to turn on the showers for bathing, for the approximate 8,000 victims. Shortly thereafter the camp was emptied of the Jewish prisoners who were transported in packed trains to Auschwitz for extermination.

The pattern of round ups and raids systematically by district with the collaboration of the police was working well from 1941-1944. Men, women, and children were being selected for "relocation." One day, in 1942, in the 13th century historically Jewish Marais arrondissement, the director of the Paris Police for district # 4 ordered a morning raid on the local schools. The mothers had just dropped off their children at l'Ecole Maternelle on Rue Francois Miron. Then the police stormed in, scooping up the frightened children, transporting them for extermination in Aushwitz. As a result of these police actions 12,000 innocent children perished from 1942-1944.

Adolf Eichmann met with SS Commander Dannecker to discuss the Jewish solution. Six days later Emile Hennequin, Director of the Paris City Police, on July 16, 1942 at 4:00 ordered the round up of 13,152 Jewish citizens, of which 9853 were women with children. The metro station at Quai de Grenelle, in the shadows of the Eiffel tower was closed and guarded. District 15 became its own fortified city. Jacques Doriot, as head of the Paris Fascist Party (PPF) assembled his 3,000 Nazi youth members in the Velodrome d'Hiver. This was an indoor cycling race track that now was used for fascist rallies. The glass roof to the stadium was darkly painted to disguise its impending use. Buses arrived almost all day, loaded with Jewish Parisians. People were disappearing from the streets of Paris, and not returning, like the Haskelson and Picard families.

Pierre Haskelson was a typical 5 year old boy living in Paris. His family was quite financially comfortable, and they had an apartment in the city, as well as a villa in the countryside, about 30 kilometers outside Paris. His father Jacques and grandfather Jean had a successful cutlery factory. They produced the silver chemical finishing to silverware. His mother Cecile Ullmann worked in the storefront, selling the cutlery products. They had some influential clients which would prove useful in time. Cecile's mother Rose Weill Ullmann lived with them to help care for Pierre. She enjoyed making and selling hats also. Since the 1800's, the family records show residency in Switzerland and France. Relatives from the Weill-Ullmann and Haskelson families lived nearby, and Cecile was very close to her cousin Yvonne. Pierre enjoyed playing with his cousins Francoise and Michel, Yvonne and Paul's children.

Jacques and Cecile Haskelson received a notice to report to the Préfecture de Police to register. Around the same time, the French army re-activated Jacques for a second call to service. The family did not need the food ration coupons, and they were French nationals first, religion was never an issue, so they did not want it exploited through registration. Through Jacques business contacts they were able to get identity papers without the "J" stamp for Jews. This also avoided having to wear the L'Etoile required under Nazi occupation. Jacques also handsomely bribed a priest to get three falsified Baptismal Certificates. They were given Catholic baptismal names of three dead children on the church books.

Cousins Yvonne and Paul Picard had two children to feed and were not as wealthy as their cousins, so they registered and received their food ration coupon book. It was a seemingly typical market day in the center of town, though typical is almost impossible during wartime, in an occupied country. The family of four was shopping with their coupons when suddenly the streets were closed off by trucks with Nazi armed guards. French police began checking papers and grabbing people, throwing them on trucks and buses. Paul, Yvonne, Francoise, and Michel were ordered onto one of the buses. A Christian neighbor reflexively lunged for the two children, pulling them into her body, screaming "No these are mine!" The two mothers locked eyes, Yvonne nodded, and the buses left. That would be the last time anyone would see the Picards. The brave neighbor rushed the six year old Francoise and the 10 year old Michel into her church. The priest was able to place the children with two families. Michel, as a boy, was needed to help on a farm. The family unfortunately kept him in servitude, working hard, long hours. Francoise was placed in a loving Christian home and attended Catholic school. Both safe homes were in Nancy, about 280 kilometers east of Paris.

Jacques Haskelson had to report to the French Army to defend the southern border from the German invasion. Fearing for his family's safety, he and Cecile made an escape plan. They were one of the few families still owning a car. Jacques had been buying as much gasoline as possible, hiding it in the villa barn.

*Haskelson family with Car, 1940 France. Courtesy of Pierre Haskelson.*

The night he left for service, he and Cecile made one more plan. The time had come, Pierre's mother and grandmother packed the car, including Rose's handmade hats, and they fled south into the French countryside. As dawn broke, Cecile heard trucks approaching on the road followed by blaring German air raid sirens. She pulled the car behind some shrubbery and told Pierre to jump off the road into a ditch to hide. Pierre, now 6 years old, heard and felt the pain of his arm breaking. Next to him laid a dead horse, victim of the German Stukas, dive bombers. When it was safe, the three continued driving away from Paris. Ahead was an army hospital. At first the doctors refused to treat Pierre, but Cecile "negotiated" with them. It is unclear whether she used a hidden gemstone from the hem of her skirt, or offered anything else to the army doctors, but Pierre remembers a very assertive mother fighting for his care. His arm was set in a cast and placed in a sling.

It seems incredulous to find humor as one is fleeing from the Nazis, but on the way to Bordeaux, they stopped to picnic. Grandma Rose was wearing one of her famous hats, sitting on the ground facing Pierre. Cecile and son burst out in laughter as a cow snuck up behind her and proceeded to eat her hat for lunch. Off they went to Bordeaux.

The second Haskelson plan was if Jacques could get released from service when the Germans withdrew from the southern front, he would make his way to Bordeaux. In the center square was a kiosk pillar where notices were posted. There it was the notice from her husband and where he was staying. The family united and headed by boat to North Africa, to Medea, Algeria. Pierre attended Catholic school, along with several Green Shirt Nazi youth members. There was little work and the family was running out of money. Jacques desperately tried to immigrate to Switzerland and Argentina, but countries had immigration quotas and there were many fleeing refugees and Nazis. In 1942, the family decided to relocate to the larger city of Algiers.

While looking for work, Jacques heard of a meeting of the Jewish Resistance Underground at the Hotel Aleti. The Force Francaise de L'Interieur ( FFI) needed translators. Fluent in German, French, and English, he was needed to intercept Hitler's speeches and short wave radio coded Nazi messages. The FFI imbedded Jacques in the Vichy newspaper office where he had access to the Nazi messages. He was able to translate the transmissions to the FFI headquarters. Once again, Jacques made good choices and useful future contacts.

Still at risk as a hidden Jew in a war zone, the family was almost killed one night. The nightly sirens wailed warning the Haskelsons to run down six flights of stairs to the bomb shelter in the basement of their apartment building. It was hard to tell who was dropping the bombs, but the building was hit, killing half the residents. Covered in blood and debris a petrified 8 year old Pierre heard his parents say *Grace a Dieu, Thanks to God!*

After the Americans landed in North Africa, life improved for the Haskelsons. Because of Jacques work with the FFI, he was one of the first to hear the war had ended. He took his son to the apartment rooftop and they watched the American tracer rockets light the sky as they bombed the remaining German ships in the allied controlled port. Pierre reported in an interview: "That was the night I found out I was a Jew."

Life got better for the family in Algiers. They opened a successful wine store, which Pierre helped in after school. Pierre was an outstanding student and a member of a local Boy Scout club. Cecile hosted dinner parties for former FFI friends including Jacques supervisor General Marc Clark. Grandma Rose decided it was time to be repatriated to her native Switzerland.

In 1946, Jacques correctly predicted the political changes coming to Algeria. He felt the French would be forced out of Algiers soon. Once again trying to protect his family, Jacques asked his friend General Clark to arrange for visas to NY for the family. They boarded an army truck for a 6 hours, 200 miles trip to the port. The ship was a Navy freighter about to be mothballed upon arrival in NY. For seventeen days, 11 year old Pierre played on a military vessel. He learned some English from demobilized Navy sailors, and had his first taste of milk.

Before leaving Algiers for America, Jacques returned to Paris to retrieve family possessions. The Vichy French commission for Jewish property and local residents had confiscated the apartment, villa, cutlery store and factory. He received 1940 devaluated rate reparations in 1952 from the French government. The apartment concierge admitted hiding the Haskelson family album. For a negotiated price, she sold the album back to Jacques.

He also went looking for Michel and Francoise. He found the cousins and offered to send for them in America when settled in. But the children chose to remain in Nancy. They occasionally visited their grandmother in Switzerland on summer school vacations. Michel converted back to Judaism, attended the University and became a college professor. He is currently married to his fourth wife. Francoise remained devoutly Catholic, and became known as Sister Paula, the Jewish Nun. The trauma of the Holocaust and the dramatic loss of their parents haunt both siblings to this day. The safety of the cloistered monastery in the countryside outside Paris provides serenity for Soeur Paula.

Jacques, Cecile, and Pierre lived and worked in Queens, NY. Pierre attended college where he met Rosalyn Berger. Roz and Pierre Haskelson are the proud parents of Jean-Jacques, Michelle, and Marc. They have five grandchildren, ages 7-12, quatre petites filles et un garcon. The Haskelsons return to France often while on vacation, and meet with their cousins when possible.

In 2009, for the first time, Pierre was able to locate his grandfather's grave in the partially restored Jewish cemetery. They have also visited the Memorial de la Shoah Musee in the Marais 4th district of Paris. The ashes of some of the murdered innocents are interred there. Overwhelming is the archived collection of indexed identification cards, ordered by the Nazi controlled Vichy government, and registered by the French local police. *May they rest in peace. Qu'ils reposent en paix.*

## Chapter Six

# A Baker's Loaf of Life:
# A Generation Saved by the
# Resistance in Quaregnon, Belgium

A dear friend and I were chatting about my trip to my grandmother's ancestral Russian homeland. I knew Marcelle, or Micke as she is known to her friends, had been born in Belgium, but that country was not on my radar for this book. As casually "as pass the Belgian Beer please," Micke said, "you know my grandmother hid children in flour sacks in her bakery attic during the Holocaust."

I never know where my next research lead will come from, but this certainly was unexpected. Upon further inquiry, I discovered Marcelle's grandmother, Valerie Destrain-Discart (married-maiden) and her husband Francois, operated a *boulangerie-pâtisserie* in Quaregnon. Valerie belonged to the local Rivage parish, Eglise Saint Joseph. In 1940, the bakery was located around the corner from the church at the address 316 Rue du Rivage. Micke informed me that the building no longer existed, as a highway was built through the area.

As the story began to further unfold, I had trouble sleeping nights. I would wake up at 3am, wondering what still did exist in Quaregnon. Thanks to Google Earth and hours of internet searching, we discovered that the street and the original building were still standing. The highway was routed around the outskirts of this village, thereby saving a historic area. The street once known as Rue du Rivage was now known as Rue Paul Pastur (RPP.) Building # 316 was no longer a bakery it was now a rented residence. Further, the retired town pharmacist who is now the landlord of this building is the son of the 1940 pharmacist, Monsieur Willy Thomas, Sr. I had to do everything in my power to control myself and not hop on a plane to Belgium. Did the attic still exist above #316 Rue Paul Pastur?

The next night I awoke suddenly with the overwhelming need to locate one of the hidden children of Quaregnon. I contacted domestic and international

organizations, searched the internet, and spoke with generous people throughout the world. In the fall of 2009, I received a telephone call from Mr. Joseph
Loeb, a hidden child of Quaregnon. He had been informed by my contact at
the United States Holocaust Memorial Museum in Washington, DC that I
was looking for him. The next twelve months brought a flood of memories to
Micke, Jose, Willy Jr, and the surviving resistance fighters of the righteous
southern Belgium town of Quaregnon.

The history of the Jews in the region now known as Belgium, can be traced
back to the great first Diaspora. The Roman destruction of the second great
temple in Jerusalem in 70 C.E. led to one of the earliest movements of the
Israelites from Judea. The Jewish Diaspora to Europe and the Netherlands was
at times welcomed and other times resented. Thirteenth century Belgium has
evidence of Jewish headstones and "Rue des Juifs." As in other countries, the
history of acceptance and expulsion over the centuries was dependent on the
ruling monarchy. The crusades were particularly hard for Jews, the choice was
Christian baptism or death. The ruling monarch Duke John II favored the Jews
and allowed the community to practice Judaism openly. Unfortunately it was
short lived with the devastating Black Plague. Jews were burned at the stake as
somehow being the devils that inflicted the populace with the deadly disease.

Some Marranos, or Spanish secret Jews, fleeing the 15th century Spanish
Inquisition settled in Antwerp, using their skills as traders of precious gems.
As Austria ruled Belgium in 1713, Jews were able to cross borders forming
more communities. Even during Napoleon's brief rule of Belgium, Jews
could practice their religion. By 1831, Belgium regained its independence
from Dutch control and Judaism was one of the state recognized religions,
along with the sometimes tense relationship between the Dutch Protestants
and the Catholics. Yiddish and Flemish were spoken in the northern regions;
French and Yiddish in the southern parts of Belgium. King Leopold I would
be credited with building the first rail system connecting Brussels with Mechelen (Malines) which later would prove fateful for the Jews. Jews fleeing
from the Russian Pogroms in the 19th century also found a welcome home
in Belgium and the Netherlands. The rise in antisemitism in Poland and the
defeat of democracy in 1933 by Hitler's Nazi Fascist government brought the
last and largest immigration of Jews to Belgium.

Belgium was occupied by Germany during both WWI and WWII, in spite
of its efforts to remain neutral. The initial resistance movement was formed
during the First World War. The poppy fields of Flanders are witness to the
loss of Belgian and Allied soldiers' lives. In May 1940, Germany invaded
Belgium occupying it until its defeat by Allied forces in 1945. King Leopold
III was taken hostage shortly after he sent a letter in 1942 to Hitler asking
for protection of the Jews of Belgium. The largest Jewish populations were

located in Antwerp and Brussels. In 1939, there were approximately 90,000 Jews throughout Belgium. By 1945, less than half, or 40,000 had survived the Holocaust. The Nazis looted the diamond industry which never recovered to pre-war status. Currently Bilingual Flemish-French Belgium is the headquarters for NATO and is one third of the Benelux Union of Belgium, Netherlands, and Luxembourg. The Jewish population of Belgium today is approximately 35,000 People.

Quaregnon Belgium is a diminutive town located 74 kilometers south of Brussels and 10 km west of Mons. The creation of the town's name has been attributed to an architect who when asked to build structures proclaimed "Quare Non" why not?! A more likely explanation of the name Quaregnon is its Latin and French origin of four quarters. Artifacts from the Medieval and Roman periods indicate its ancient history. The region was vibrant during the industrial period for its coal and iron mining. But visible destructive evidence from the fight against the Nazi German occupation can be seen in both the structure and economy of Quaregnon. It is a Boraine municipality located in the Walloon province of Hainaut and the district of Mons. Today the population is similar to that of during World War II, with emigration in and out of the city, holding at approximately 19,000 people. The remains of the original church of Saint Quentin tower are across from the city hall, where town historians have documented Quaregnon's bravery through two world wars. Quaregnon may be a small town, but it has a big brave heart. The people understand well *to save one child is to save all of humanity; Sauver un enfant C'est sauver toute l'humanité.*

Bruno and Hertha Salomon Loeb lived in the town of Sankt Ingbert in western Germany, bordering northeastern France. Their daughters Ruth, Hedwig (Hede) and Inge were born there. In October 1935 they left their ancestral home seeking freedom from religious persecution. Belgium had an excellent reputation of country first, religion second. If you worked hard and pledged allegiance to the country, your rights were protected, even as an immigrant. It was also known that Belgium and the Netherlands opposed Hitler's Fascist ideologies. The Loeb's thought they would be safe in their new country, and continued to celebrate life by giving birth to their fourth daughter, Hana, in Spa, Belgium in the Walloon region. Two years later Bruno finally got the son he wanted when Jose was born in Malmedy on May 5, 1938. Completing their migration northwest, the Loeb's reached their intended destination in Brussels, renting an apartment near the Royal Palace, where baby Irene was born, five months after the German occupation of Belgium on May 10, 1940.

In the years preceding the bakery, Valerie Destrain-Discart worked in the historic Earthenware factory *faiencerie de Wasmuel*, founded by Isidore Paulus in 1834. The Mouzin and Meyer family members continued the artistic productions of their relatives. The owners of this company employed many Freemasons, some of which were probably undisclosed Jews. When the Nazis invaded Wasmuel, which later was incorporated into the town of Quaregnon, they demanded the workers be deported to labor camps. Henri Meyer retooled his company from the production of artistic mantelpiece clocks to needed dinnerware for the occupiers as well as affordable items for war torn locals. By redirecting his productions, Meyer was able to make the case to the Nazis of the necessity of keeping the workers in Quaregnon in 1940.

In 1934 Valerie left the factory and with her husband Francois Destrain opened a boulangerie-patisserie at 316 Rue du Rivage. Francois was the bookkeeper and Valerie the baker. She worshipped at the nearby Rivage parish of the Eglise Saint Joseph. Completing the family was her son Marcel who was engaged to Ida Wins. The townspeople of Quaregnon, with the exception of a few collaborators hated the Nazis. They were appalled at the imposed restrictions to Jews and others perceived as a threat to the third Reich. Suffering a terrible loss of people and buildings as the little town of Quaregnon tried to hold off the invasion, a growing underground resistance movement was developing.

*Quaregnon Bakery #316 Rue du Rivage Resistance movement bakers Francois, Valerie, & Ida Destrain. Courtesy of Marcelle Destrain Gimborn.*

On May 10, 1940 Marcel Destrain, while serving in the Belgian army infantry, was arrested in the town of Nevele, near Ghent, by the Nazi SS and imprisoned in Stalag 5B in Villingen, Germany where he and other French and Belgian Prisoners of War spent four long years in a hard labor camp. Concentration Camp conditions prevailed with poor food and sanitary conditions. Strong willed Valerie took immediate action on this injustice, becoming a leader in the Belgian Resistance for the Boringe region. The base of operation would be on Rue du Rivage, #316 also known as the Bakery of Quaregnon.

Victor and Rose Lete-Faucon were active members of their community. Victor was Deputy Mayor of Quaregnon and Rose was an active member of her Rivage Parish church. After the forced occupation of the town by the Germans, Achille Faucon, brother of Rose met with her and Victor. The three became active Resistance fighters. Resistance to the Nazis came as both aggressive and passive actions. One night a significant German rail spur was bombed. No one was ever identified as the saboteur, but Achille and his team were bought a round at the pub.

In Brussels from 1940-1942, things had become intolerable for the Jews. Due to the same antisemitic Nuremberg Laws issued in Germany, Jews lost their businesses, could not attend public school, had to register with the district police, and were forced to wear the yellow Stars of David to self identify when on the streets. Harsh consequences read the notice on each apartment door would result in your failure to register detailed information of all family members on the required following form: ASSOCIATION DES JUIF EN BELGIQUE COMITE LOCAL DE BRUXELLES. A local Judenrat or Jewish council was assigned in each district to facilitate this registration making the procedure appear less threatening.

The Nazi Germans found a perfect isolated location for a *Sammellager fuer Jueden, a* collection camp for Jews. The former World War I Dossin Barracks in Mechelen was right near the railway halfway south of Antwerp and halfway north of Brussels, the two most concentrated areas where Jews lived. The residents of Mechelen (fr. Malines) were used to having German troops in the area from prior wars. Fort Breendonk a historical fortification and war prison was now reopened by the Germans as a prison camp for political opponents, resistance fighters, and prisoners of war. Most of the inmates were non-Jewish POWs. The only Jews incarcerated there were useful Jews, like a blacksmith or an accountant. The shooting wall and hanging platform behind the fort remain in evidence of what happened when a prisoner's usefulness was done.

The summer of 1942 should have been a playful time for Ruth Loeb. But she received the first family notice at age 17 to report "To Work." The *Arbeitseinsatzbefehl (AB), No.001825* was Ruth's documented *work command* or order. Failure to report would result in penalties for the remaining family, including the loss of food rations. Ruth was likely told it would be a work camp for the summer and then she could return home. She reported to the local station in Brussels and then with others was transported by train to Malines, as it is written in French Brussels, Mechelen in the Flemish region. Under heavy guard from Flemish SS Nazi collaborators, with Nazi German guards and dogs, she was now an inmate in the former Dossin Army Barracks.

Ruth was listed as No.840 on convoy I, meaning the first cattle car train packed with Jews heading to Auschwitz. Her transit document listed her profession as housekeeper, which Ruth would have expected her summer camp work to have been upon arrival. On August 4, 1942 the trains with packed cattle cars of innocent human beings left the Dossin collection center in Mechelen. It did not arrive until the next day, August 5, in Auschwitz. Ruth was very thin and the ride was oppressively hot and nauseating. Hundreds were crammed into one car with little air and a bucket for a toilet. The rail trip may have taken over 20 hours to travel the 1241 kilometers. Ruth died on September 1, 1942 of an illness in Auschwitz according the commandant's signed Sterbebucher or death certificate No. 42/26406. One must read "illness" with skepticism.

The first convoys leaving Mechelen were all filled with people who obeyed the *Arbeitseinsatzbefehl*. Reports reached Brussels and outlying towns of deaths such as Ruth's and missing Jews leaving the house in the morning to get food rations never returning home. Jews started disobeying the orders to report, forcing trucks to pull up in front of apartments for the violent *Razzias, raids* for the collection of people. The Loeb family and many others desperately searched for a way to save their children.

The *Comité de Défense des Juifs* (CDJ) is an organization that became the covert Belgian Resistance Movement during the German occupation. There were armed and unarmed branches, plus a well organized division for adults and children. Social workers, clergy consisting of nuns, priests, and cardinals, Kings and Queens, and non-Jewish ordinary citizens were all resisting the Nazis and trying to protect the Jewish victims of Belgium.

The *Kinderen,* children's division, with about 32 members was responsible for hiding and supporting those who had gone underground. From 1942-1944 about 3,500 children were saved from deportation by unarmed resistors. These were *enfants caches* children hidden in Christian homes and in convents. "With Germany we step many degrees downward and reach the lowest possible depths," said Cardinal van Roey, Roman Catholic Archbishop of Malines, Belgium in a speech at Wavre-Notre Dame. "We have a duty of conscience to combat and to strive for the defeat of these dangers. . . . Reason and good sense both direct us towards confidence, towards resistance" (Dec.15, 1941).

Sister Marie Amélie in a convent nearby the Mechelen deportation center hid Jewish girls, issuing them baptismal certificates to protect their identities.

"They are the chosen children of God, we are responsible to save them," said some Pastors. She worked with CDJ Social Workers Jeanne-Ida Sterno and Andree Geulen. They also appealed to Elisabeth, the Queen Mother of Belgium, who publically encouraged Belgians to do all they could to help the Jews, especially to save the children.

Bruno and Hertha Loeb sought the help of the CDJ in hiding their children. The adults were too difficult to hide, but children were easier, especially if they had less Jewish features. Hiding an entire family together was impossible and dangerous, so they always had to be split up. The hope was if the parents survived, they would reunite them after the camps were liberated. Hana and Jose at age six and four years old were the likely first choices to go into hiding. They were already potty trained yet had a child's innocence of what was happening, so they could not reveal information if questioned by the Gestapo or local fascist police. The CDJ social worker strangely left the Loeb's and went to the bakery in Brussels. A nun came in to purchase a loaf of bread. After a brief stay in a convent Hana was living in the home of the Sleeger family and was given the name of Jeanine, the same name as Madame Sleeger.

The same procedure was repeated south of Brussels in Quaregnon. Rose Faucon was actively finding homes with the resistance for Jewish children in southern Belgium. When contacted by the CDJ in 1942 to find a safe home for a little four year old boy from Brussels, Rose decided to temporarily adopt Jose Loeb. Victor altered City Hall records, finding a child who had died with a similar birth date, and added Jose Lete as his registered birth child, joining two other Lete children Edgard and Blanche. Edgard was exactly ten years older than Jose, both born on May 5.

*Edgard Lete & Jose, 1943, ages 15 & 5, Quaregnon, Belgium. Courtesy of Jose Loeb.*

Under cover of night, a CDJ social worker and a resistance fighter entered the darkened bakery on Rue du Rivage # 316. Once inside the bakery, a child was exposed from under a coat. The baker led them all up two levels above the store, climbing narrow wooden stairs with no railings. Furniture partially blocked a narrow right turn leading to a door. Past the door was the steepest staircase of all. Ascending to the attic, they found the burlap sacks as expected. Hidden guns and rifles were removed from the burlap sacks, and the child placed inside. Earlier that day, the nuns from both the Protestant and Catholic churches had come to Valerie Discart's Bakery for their loaves of bread. The safe house families knew who to expect at what time as they enjoyed their daily mealtime bread.

One little boy was not so little and could not hide in a bakery attic flour sack. Samuel Rozenberg was nine years old when he had to be separated from his parents to be saved. His first safe house returned him to the social worker during one follow up visit. Samuel was having a terrible adjustment. Alain and Lea Urbain Pierart members of the Protestant church agreed to accept the boy. The resistance in Quaregnon found the name of a dead baptized boy named Paul. Safe house families never knew who and where the others lived. They may have suspected, but it was never discussed for the safety of all. Solange Pierart was 16 at the time of Paul's arrival and the two bonded quickly. There was an unspoken understanding of her sudden new little brother's arrival. Occasionally Solange was asked to deliver and pick up papers in sealed envelopes around town. Sometimes they would contain food and clothing ration tickets to help support the hidden children.

One day Victor Lete packed a satchel containing loaves of bread and falsified documents and government seals. He boarded a train station heading east to the French border. Suddenly, the train stopped and shouts and dogs barking were followed by the Nazi SS boarding the train to inspect papers. Some passengers jumped off the train trying to escape the attack dogs and shooting SS troops. Using the diversion of this chaos, Victor hid the fake identification papers and document seals he was carrying in the hollowed out loaves of bread. The resistance was able to secure the passage for many important Jewish people as a result of the *LOAVES OF LIFE*. One such person was Paul Henocq the head Rabbi of Belgium. Rose hid the Rabbi, his wife and parents while her husband secured their safe passage out of the country. Victor received numerous honors after the war for his dangerous resistance work.

On August 27, 1943, Hede Loeb, age 16 was walking back to her apartment, when the loud sirens screeched and the trucks came. She hid behind a dumpster and watched her remaining family be taken away. She could not enter her apartment. The concierge would turn her in to the Gestapo. She lived on the streets for awhile before being taken in by a family as a domestic. Bruno age 44, Hertha age 42, Inge age 11, and Irene age 3 were taken to Kazerne Dossin, the barrack waiting rooms of death in Mechelen. The four Loebs numbers 411, 412, 413, and 414 left the *Sammellager*, the transit camp on cattle car train convoy number XXIIA, arriving in Auschwitz on September 22. They were all victims of Hitler's Endlösung, Final Solution.

Marcel Destrain was able to escape from Stag 5B crossing the border into Switzerland where he spent three months recovering. The resistance helped him get back to Quaregnon on October 27, 1944. Now married, Marcel and Ida Destrain-Wins, living with heroic Valerie and François above the Bakery, gave birth to Marcelle exactly one year later.

The return of hidden children after the war was very controversial. The Catholic church initially wanted baptized children to remain with their Catholic families or in the convent orphanages. Survivors and relatives in America and countries worldwide protested. The church recanted its recommendation and agencies such as HIAS, the Hebrew Immigrant Aid Society proceeded to reunite hidden children, parents, and relatives. Although well meaning, this arrangement was a nightmare for many Jewish hidden children and their rescuer parents.

Paul Pierart's parents survived Auschwitz and after months of recovery returned to the Hainaut region. His sister died in Auschwitz. The transition from his loving safe rescuer family to his natural parents was difficult at first. Arrangements were made for Paul to spend weekends with Lea, Alain, and Solange Pierart, while living during the week with the Rozenbergs. One Sunday while Lea bathed her adopted son, Paul stood up and screamed "call me Samuel, I am Samuel Rozenberg!" For Lea it was like a knife in her heart, she knew she had lost her son. To this day Solange tells this story with tears in her eyes. Samuel Rozenberg joined a cousin living in Rio De Janeiro and became a successful cardiologist. He is married with four children. His first daughter is named Solange in honor of his adopted big sister who saved his life. Samuel speaks to Solange Pierart on the telephone often and returns to Quaregnon annually for a visit with her. The *Righteous Among the Nations* Medal and Certificate of Honor was awarded to the Pierart family in 1994 at The Yad Vashem Holocaust Martyrs and Heroes Remembrance Authority in Jerusalem, Israel.

Max Loeb, brother of Bruno, had left Germany before him and after a brief stay in Luxembourg moved to America in 1937. After the war, Max submitted forms to HIAS searching for any surviving family. The CDJ informed them where Jeanine and Jose had been hidden. Hede knew the location of her surviving siblings and when it was safe the resistance arranged for her to visit with Jeanine and Jose a few times during the two years in hiding. Uncle Max filed for custody of the three surviving children in 1947 to take them to New York City.

Jose Lete as a little four year old was safely sheltered, often unaware of the drama all around him in Quaregnon. Edgard walked him to school, Rose took him to church. He and friends played with the rabbits in the cages behind the house on Rue de Paul Pastur, unaware that the bunnies sometimes became his dinner. Now at age 9, Jose was forced to leave the Lete family to be given to relatives that really were strangers. Maman Lete was devastated; Jose and Edgard were her two beloved sons. This was Jose's family and home and it was painful for him to leave. Rose and Jose truly loved each other as mother and son. When told he would be leaving soon for America, Jose ran away from home, later found by Victor. The separation was very traumatic, leaving permanent emotional scars on all. Madame Rose Lete-Faucon wrote to her son Jose shortly after his arrival in NY, on the occasion of his 10th birthday. This letter and some photographs are what Jose cherishes to this day as a 72 year old man. Jose Lete Loeb is a successful pharmacist and a graduate of Fordham University in NY. He is a kind gracious generous man giving to several organizations that help orphans and oppressed people worldwide. Jeanine Loeb Strauss and her husband, also a survivor live in California and have two sons and three grandchildren. They have visited with her rescue family in Brussels often over the years.

Thanks to the internet and worldwide agencies, I have been able to communicate with amazingly generous people like Evelyn Handel, a child survivor in Liege. It was Evelyn who connected me to hidden child agencies. Finding Monsieur Willy Thomas in Quaregnon was another piece of the growing puzzle of discoveries of untold, uplifting Holocaust stories. Clearly the town of Quaregnon is a very special place. The Belgian Resistance Movement against the mighty Nazi Germans saved many citizens. The courage of a little town and its righteous Christian people is a testament to what can be done when we stand up to tyranny. During my separate interviews with Edgard Lete and Solange Pierart in Quaregnon, I asked them why they and their parents would risk everything, including their lives to save a Jewish child. They looked strangely at me, finding the question odd. They responded: "Why wouldn't we?" *and* "To save a child, how could we not do anything?" Love and humanity have no borders. *L'amour et L'Humanité n'ont pas de Frontières,* A. Auquier (1994) Historian, Quaregnon

Unfortunately even with heroic efforts like witnessed in Brussels and Quaregnon, more than 25,000 Belgian Jews died during the Holocaust. Meticulous record keeping of registrations and numbered deportation transit orders by the Germans reflect the mentality of order, organization, and detail. The Nazis by their own hand have allowed us to be witness to the horrors and fate of the 6 million murdered Jewish men, woman, and children. Between August 1942 and July 1944, the date of the last recorded Mechelen to Auschwitz

Convoy XXVI, 24,916 Jews and 351 gypsies were deported. Only 1,221 of these deportees survived.

On May 25, 2010 I arrived in Brussels and traveled to Mechelen to the *The Jewish Museum* of *Deportation and Resistance (JMDR)* (*Joods Museum van Deportatie en Verzet.*) Many of the documents I am grateful to continue to have access to are in Flemish or French, so thank you *Google Translator* and the documentation staff at JMDR. The courtyard behind the museum has a lovely garden gathering area. The barracks are now rented apartments. I was pleased to see students from a secondary school visiting the museum to study the Holocaust.

Next day I traveled to Quaregnon, Belgium. My French-Flemish train directionality from north to south aside, not to mention a bomb threat on the return train ride, May 26, 2010 was one of the most incredible days of my life. The weather was dismal, cold and rainy, but I hardly noticed it until I saw my photographs later showing my water stained blouse. I was met at the Quaregon train station by Willy Thomas, the town historian and Michele Messine, a retired teacher and excellent interpreter. After many emails across the Atlantic in French and English, and with the help of my also sleepless friend Micke, they planned an incredible journey for me. I met with Edgard Lete and Solange Pierart who are octogenarians, but reverted back to being teenage resistance fighters during my emotional interviews with them. I met Guy Roland, the current Mayor of Quaregnon and shared my research about his heroic town. Then the overwhelming moment came to enter #316 Rue Paul Pastur, formerly Rue du Rivage. The current renter of the house was unaware of the history of this building and graciously allowed Willy, Edgard, Michele, and myself to traipse through her home. We ascended the stairs to the attic retracing the very steps described in this chapter. As I stood in the attic moving to the corners where the burlap flour sacks of hidden guns and children had preceded me, I was overwhelmed to tears, as I am now writing this ending. Thank you, Thank you, Merci Beaucoup Marcelle Gimborn-Destrain for sharing your family story with me. Thank you also to all the survivors and rescuers mentioned in this chapter. I hope this book in part honors the memory of your family members.

To the memory of Valerie Destrain-Discart, the Baker of Quaregnon and the heroic, yet very humble people of Quaregnon, it was an honor to visit your town. You truly understand to save one child is to save all of humanity; Sauver un enfant C'est sauver toute l'humanité.

## Chapter Seven

# Shattered Childhoods in Hiding: Dutch Resistors, a Baron, and a Fairytale Castle

Someone stole Jesus! Two days before Christmas, 1942, in South Holland, the baby Jesus statue was missing from the church manger. As quietly as the statue had disappeared, so it had returned in time for the holiday. Allegedly, a Jewish hidden child feared for the life of baby Jesus when he heard the Christ child was born Jewish. Thus like himself, Jesus became a hidden Jewish child, victim of the Nazi occupation of the Netherlands.

There were small numbers of early Jewish settlers in the Netherlands during the Roman period. Larger Jewish communities developed, with their own health and dietary laws. Over the centuries, Jews were welcomed or expelled at a King's discretion. Jewish expulsions and murders were very high during the Black Plague of 1349. The fact that fewer Jews were getting sick and dying due to their religious rituals, was not understood by the populace, hence they were blamed for the epidemic. Writings by the Catholic Church blaming the Jews for the death of Jesus also fueled antisemitism.

In Spain Jews, Muslims, and Protestants were being forced to convert to Catholicism. Failure to do so resulted in burning at the stake. Many Jewish astronomers, doctors, and bankers became "Conversos," converted but secretly continued to practice their religion. It was a Jewish banker in 1492 that helped finance the voyage from Spain of Christopher Columbus. Shortly thereafter, the Spanish Monarchy under pressure from the church began the Spanish Inquisition. Some Jews chose to remain and become Catholic others fled the country mainly to the Netherlands. This became the base community of Marranos, Sephardic Jews from Spain and Portugal. They were extremely important in Amsterdam and in the port city of Rotterdam, as the Dutch West Indies and Dutch East Trade routes opened. The Spanish speaking Jewish immigrants were multilingual merchants and doctors, with many international contacts, that were needed to grow trade and commerce in the Netherlands.

The Yiddish speaking Ashkenazi Jews began emigrating around 1630 from Eastern Europe and Germany. They settled in what became a Jewish Quarter in Amsterdam, open to non-Jews, especially book printers and artists such as Rembrandt. Census records indicate Jewish teachers in the Hague and Haarlem also. One of the most lucrative industries to this day in the Netherlands is the Diamond Trade, a skill that Jews advanced working with precious stones before the Diaspora from the Ottoman Empire. The port city of Antwerp became an important trade route for the Dutch Diamond Trade by the Jews into the twentieth century. Following the French revolution and independence of the Netherlands respectively, in the 18th and 19th centuries, Jews adopted Dutch as their primary language and became assimilated Dutch citizens in secular Holland and the greater Netherlands.

In 1940, Germany occupied the Netherlands, to the outrage of the secular, politically anti-war neutral government. One and a half percent of the population was Jewish, or about 140,000 people. As they did in Europe, the Fascist Germans enacted the Nuremberg Laws imposing restrictions on Dutch Jews, and waging a violent antisemitic discriminatory campaign against them. By 1942, the Nazis, along with Dutch collaborators, had begun the containment and deportation of Jews from all the providences of Holland to the Westerbork Transit Camp, and/or directly to Auschwitz and Sobibor, in Poland. At the end of the war, in 1946, thanks to the brave Dutch Resistance Fighters 30,000 Jews had survived. These non-Jewish members of the resistance, risked their lives hiding Jewish children and families, in order "to do the right thing." Sadly, 80% of the Jewish population of the Netherlands was decimated.

Anne Frank, Ruth Jacobsen, Fred Lessing were all children growing up in Germany. Their fathers all lost their businesses with the enactment of the Nuremberg Laws preventing Jews from owning businesses and property. All three families fled to the Netherlands, to Amsterdam, Delft, and South Holland to escape Nazi persecution. All three young children went into hiding, protected by non-Jews in the Dutch Resistance Movement.

Fred Lessing was four years old when the Germans occupied Holland. Forced to wear the Yellow Star of David daily, he, his brother and parents were daily targets of antisemitic ridicule. His favorite comfort toy was his bear, aptly named Bear. Two years later, six year old Fred and his family went into hiding, but in different safe homes in Delft, secured by the Dutch Resistance. The family had to be split up; it would be too dangerous to hide all the Lessings in one place. Fred became a good little Christian boy for the next two years. Bear, also in hiding with Fred suffered a terrible trauma when his head was bitten off by a Nazi German Sheppard dog. One night, Fred's mother was allowed a secret visit to her son. Told of Bear's injury, she fashioned a head from her son's coat pocket.

The well respected, educated, upper class assimilated Frank family left Germany in 1933 after the democratic Weimar government was defeated by the elected Fascist party. A series of anti Jewish decrees signaled Otto Frank it was time to leave Frankfurt. In 1933 he established the Opekta fruit extract company, which became very successful and expanded to a second company making preservative spices. Daughters Annelies Marie, Margot, and wife Edith joined Otto in Amsterdam in 1934. The girls had many school friends and the Frank family was assimilated into Dutch society. Germany occupied the Netherlands in 1940 and in order to save his company, Mr. Frank signed his company over to his trusted managers, but still covertly ran operations. It was these trusted colleagues who would hide the Frank family from 1942-1944 in the Secret Annex, Het Achterhuis, a hidden back house attic above the factory and main house, where the trusted heroic Miep Gies would later find Anne's dairy.

Ruth Jacobsen was born in 1932, in the small town of Old Frankenberg, Germany. Her family owned a shoe store in Old Frankenberg and lived a comfortable middle class life until 1937, when Ruth's mother Paula was forced to sell the business to the German government for way below its true value. The loss of income from the shoe store forced the family to move from their suburban home near her grandparents to an apartment in Dusseldorf.

On November 9th, 1938, the landlady notified Ruth's family that the Nazis planned to raid all Jewish homes that evening and round up men, women and even children. The family was petrified and feared returning home; instead, they walked the streets all night and witnessed the horrors of the raid. In utter pandemonium, glass, furniture and even human beings were seen thrown from building to the ground. Ruth was frightened by the Night of Broken Glass, Kristallnacht.

Ruth's parents, Paula and Walter, knew it was not safe to stay in Dusseldorf. Her grandparents had often vacationed at a German spa frequented by the Dutch Baron and Baroness Van Tuyll van Serooskerken from Oud Zuilen, Holland. As the situation became worse for the Jacobsens, the Baron generously offered rooms in his home for Ruth, Walter, and Paula. Ruth's grandfather was too ill to travel at this time so he and the grandmother remained in Dusseldorf. To avoid looking suspicious, the Jacobsens wore two layers of clothing taking very little else with them. Ruth and her beloved doll Ellen silently boarded a train to Holland.

Since they were going to live with Dutch Royalty, Paula gave her daughter a quick lesson on the train about formal manners, including curtseying. Upon arrival at the train station, the family was greeted by the chauffeured limousine embellished with the Baron's family crest. Ruth thought she was in a fairytale when the car approached the 13th century medieval castle, Slot Zuylen, complete with a moat!

While living briefly in the castle, Ruth was able to enjoy a childhood fantasy unaware of its uniqueness. She enjoyed taking nature walks through the park and seeing colorful flowers and small animals. She enjoyed alternating between playing war on the huge, dark staircases of the castle with the boys, and playing in the dollhouse with the Baron's daughters. Ruth found ways of retaliating when teased by the Baron's children. The mischievous placement of a spider inside the dollhouse was all it took to send the children screaming. Ruth was known to drive the local bridge keeper crazy leaping across the opening drawbridge over the Vecht River. She enjoyed hearing English, Dutch, Flemish and German spoken at invited guest dinners. After a few weeks it became unsafe to remain in the castle. Not only did the Baron hide Jewish families in the castle, but occasionally officers of the Nazi Army would stay overnight as well. There were times when Jewish families would be on the third floor, and right below on the second floor were Nazis. For safety, families were never told about each other and no one discussed religion. As is typical in the Netherlands, Nation comes first. The children were especially told nothing; these were just children needing a temporary place to stay as they passed through their village.

The Baron, his brother, and other Dutch Royal family members were part of the Dutch Resistance. Generous funds, hidden weapons, safe houses, and dangerous covert missions continued throughout the war. The Baron's son was imprisoned during the war in case the Germans needed him as collateral. The Jacobsens were relocated from the castle to a furnished safe house nearby, complete with a garden of fragrant marigolds. The family of fourteen living in the house next door provided plenty of playmates, but Beppie became her best friend. Ruth blended well in school with her bright blue eyes and fluency in Dutch. Her house was right next door to the school so after school classmates could cut through the fence to play on her swings.

News of advancing German troops into Holland meant nowhere was safe. As the family prepared to leave for America in May 1940, port Rotterdam was bombed, canceling all visas abroad. German troops marched through the village, right past the drawn shades of the Jacobsen house. As they sang German songs, Ruth was reminded of her earlier childhood.

When Ruth's grandfather died of a stroke in 1941, her grandmother came to live with them in Holland. She was with them for almost a year when she received, as did several other Jewish immigrants, a letter requesting her to register at the German occupied Dutch police office. Since it was cosigned by someone that had a Jewish name, she decided that it was safe for her to go. The Nazi trick worked, all those who reported that day were packed onto a train and deported to the death camps. Ruth's grandmother died in transit to Auschwitz.

All Jews were forced to wear the yellow Star of David when out in public. Ruth could no longer attend the school right next to her house. Children could no longer come over to play. She had to ride a public bus to Utrecht, south of Oud Zuilen, to go to a Jewish run school. It was cold with little shelter in the winter. One day was particularly bad when the Dutch Green Shirt Nazi Youth boarded her return bus. Although the bus was not full the boys forcefully demanded that Ruth give up her seat. She was in such shock she could not move. No one said a word, then finally a lady motioned for Ruth to come sit on her lap. Ruth was so humiliated and frightened she remained silent, never even telling her parents what happened.

Ruth began to notice that each day there were fewer children in her Jewish day school class. She mentioned this to her parents who asked her to count each day the number of children and when it reached less than half, she could stay home. She counted the stars, sadly the day came too soon, and missing school was not as pleasurable as expected. A week later Walter, Paula, Ruth and her doll Ellen went into hiding in an attic of a nearby safe house.

Cees van Bart, brother of Ruth's friend Beppie, was a member of the Dutch Resistance. He heard of an impending house to house raid by fascist police seeking hidden Jews. The family had to move quickly. This time, they would have to be separated. It was easier to hide Dutch speaking and looking Ruth in plain sight with a Christian family, but her parents did not have the same options. The Resistance trained Ruth how to survive in hiding. She was to think before speaking, not to ask questions, understand that the host family's children come first, and that any chores asked of her were a privilege of staying alive. At age ten, her second childhood ended.

In order to further protect Ruth the resistance changed her name to Truusje. Over the next year she would stay in many safe houses and have to learn a new last name and a new story for each. She was someone's niece, or the daughter of a church member who died. She became the best actress, playing many roles, while becoming increasingly emotionally detached for self preservation.

> Each time I was placed in a new home I would have to learn all about the family's background so I could step into their life and assume a new identity. It was hard not to confuse the details of all the families. My last name would change as I moved from family to family, but to make it a little easier for me I would be allowed to keep one first name. Ruth sounded too biblical and might have raised suspicions about my religion, so I had to choose a new first name. I chose Truusje, a good Dutch name. I became her and left Ruth in another life. (Jacobsen 2001)

*Ruth as child self portrait collage. Courtesy of Jacobsen, Ruth. Rescued Images: Memories of a Childhood in Hiding. NY: Mikaya Press. (2001).*

Some parts of her life were simple, the Nazis and their Dutch collaborators were bad, the Allies and the Dutch Resistance were good. Some homes were better than others. One train ride led her to a safe house in Amsterdam. The righteous family asked their children to share their Christmas presents with Truusje, who just appeared at their door like an angel. Although she could not attend school, a least Truusje could play outside in the fresh air, unlike another nearby Jewish hidden girl named Anne.

The Resistance always knew where Truusje was staying and tried to arrange secret visits with her parents when it was safe. Truusje visited with her parents in the town of Roemond, in South East Holland. They were hidden 24 hours each day in an attic the size of a large closet, with a bed, chair and table. The reunited family played card games, but had to be silent so as not to be heard by others in the house below. During one weekend visit Paula stepped heavily on the attic floor and the children below heard the noise. The safe house mother came up with a clever cover story. Anytime her own children misbehaved, she told them the boogeyman in the attic was coming. She used a broom to poke the ceiling, which was the signal for Walter to stomp his feet. The plan worked well for all.

The Resistance moved Truusje to the home of a childless couple. They asked her to call them Tante Hanny and Oom Jan. Jan was an elementary school teacher and he would bring Truusje toys, marbles, and books from school. But missing were other eleven year olds to play with. At Oom Jan and Tante Hanny's house Truusje was able to go outside. She enjoyed feeding the family rabbits and picking dandelions for them. Tante Hanny was a lonely housewife who confided some mature and uncomfortable marital things with Truusje. Truusje learned never to complain and be grateful to be in a safe house. But one incident left her no choice. Truusje had been bathing herself for years, but Tante Hanny enjoyed having a child she could bathe. One day the washing turned into a massage and in a reflexive rage Truusje splashed Hanny with the water. She never bathed her charge again.

Uncle Jan had a short wave radio in the garage. He would listen to Radio Orange, the Dutch Resistance channel, and report the news at the dinner table. They heard the Allied and British Troops were near. But even as the Germans were losing the war Hitler's Nazis continued their Final Solution to rid the world of Jews. A door to door raid was planned in south Holland. Truusje had to be moved out of town. She returned after the raid, but could no longer play outdoors. Even when others evacuated during the air raids, she had to remain hidden inside.

Her next safe home had many children, of the Protestant faith. Ironically, the oldest son was named Harm. He took his role seriously protecting Truusje and another Jewish hidden child, as well as his own siblings. There was hardly enough food to feed everyone and the children slept together in a large attic. For the first time, Truusje felt all the children were treated equally and she was not as lonely as she was in the other homes. Although mainly told to stay indoors, after one snowstorm she was allowed to join the other children to play outside in the innocence and purity of the newly fallen snow. Truusje longed to remain in this home, but she knew not to become attached to anyone. So she was not surprised to find herself on the way to the next home.

Resistance member Peter briefed her on her newest identity. She was now Truss de Bruin. All the adults were part of the Resistance. Peter notified Ruth that she was now living close to her parent's current location. He was eager to set up a visit, but was concerned that any one of the three might try to meet on their own, endangering them all. The visit was arranged for the evening trying to disguise the location and route so if Truusje was interrogated she really did not know her parents location. But everyday Truusje walked the family's daughter to school and then walked the streets until it was time to pick her up again. So Truusje knew the streets of Roermond very well.

Aware now that Ruth was located nearby, Paula and Walter set up a plan to see each other weekly. Truusje had mixed feelings about this. She was a sophisticated street survivor, in many ways much more savvy about survival than her parents. She knew their plan was a great risk. Nevertheless, Truusje respected her parents' emotional request and honored their plan. As Truusje passed Paula & Walters' safe house at a designated time, her father would appear in the bathroom window. If it was safe, they would wave to each other, if there was danger, she would raise her eyebrows, signaling her father to hide. This risk was worth knowing their daughter was well. These impersonal meetings provided the family with the most interaction they had in two years. Truusje constantly worried that she would not make it in time for their meetings and the grief she would cause. This new responsibility brought a new anxiety upon her already stressful existence. Life was in many ways simpler when she was dissociated emotionally and physically from her parents.

The day she dreaded happened. She passed the window and her father was not there. She continued walking and noticed a strange woman wearing what looked like her mother's dress. Peter came a few days later to let Truusje know her parents had to flee after the police searched that home looking not for Jews, but for black market goods that the host family was trading. At great risk to all involved, a resistance member agreed to shelter all the three Jacobsens, moving them further south in Holland. The family lived in large development in Brunssum, a village located only thirty minutes west of the German border. These homes were intended for the Germans staying in Holland and for Dutch relatives of Germans. Ironically it made this location a safe place to hide. Truusje knew how to hide in plain sight, which was especially important not knowing which new friends were children of Nazi officers in this housing development.

The Jacobsens reunion as a family again was awkward for Truusje. Her pale, physically and mentally fragile parents were strangers to her after two and a half long years in hiding. She felt guilty having these thoughts and emotions, so she tried to remember how she longed to be part of a family at some of the safe houses. She joined her parents for dinner with the host family, which was a very unique opportunity. If there was a knock at the door, the Jacobsen's would grab their plates and run to their hiding places within the house. One night a neighbor simply walked into the house unannounced. Walter dove under the table, leaving the hostess to explain that he was prone to anxiety from the war. Truusje's world was larger than her parents, as she was allowed outside and they remained hidden indoors. This limited their conversations and Truusje failed to emotionally reconnect with her parents. Her self-protective skills remained intact, but sometimes added to her loneliness.

In September 1944 the townspeople of Brunssum lined the streets, the possibility of German snipers still hiding no longer phased them. The liberation parade had begun. The tanks rolled through the streets with Canadian, British, and American serviceman throwing candy and cigarettes. The Jacobsens had survived the Holocaust and were allowed to choose any abandoned German home to live in as part of the Allied and Dutch war reparations agreement. The trauma of years in hiding was apparent in certain behaviors, such as always keeping a suitcase packed, even in their new home in Heerlen.

Radio Canada Broadcast April 14, 1945: After years of occupation and deprivation, the people of Holland finally have something to cheer about: liberation. Town by town, the Canadian army is pushing the Germans out of the Netherlands, freeing the Dutch and bringing the war closer to its conclusion. But there is anger alongside the euphoria. Citizens bent on revenge are publicly shearing off the hair of Dutch women who were Nazi collaborators.

Walter found a job working in an American kitchen. It was a good job and he was able to bring home lots of leftover food. When the Americans left, Walter had trouble finding work as his German accent resulted in many slammed doors. Truusje became Ruth (Ruut) again and returned to school. Thanks to her safe house teacher Oom Jan, she was placed only one grade level behind in school. She attended a quality Catholic school in Southern Holland. Ruth had very little clothing and was especially missing socks. A nun noticed the sockless former hidden child and asked Ruth's classmates to bring in one ball of yarn each. Sister Angele knitted socks for Ruth, but since not one hank of yarn was the same color, Ruth had the most colorful socks in class.

The British army remained in Holland after the Americans and Canadians left. Soldiers moved into the Brunsum development and into homes with local families. A lieutenant from Scotland, Jimmy, was assigned to the Jacobsen house. Jimmy was from Glasgow, married and a father of one boy born while he was away in service. Jimmy worked for the army during the day, and Ruth waited up at night to hear his stories. It helped her learn English too. Lieutenant Jimmy loved the movies and invited Ruth to go with him. For the first time in years she felt special. But there remained pockets of German resistance, still fighting to the death as Hitler had commanded right before his own suicide on April 30, 1945. Jimmy reluctantly returned to the front again. Upon his leave, Jimmy wrote a note in Ruth's school book:

She is a winsome wee thing, She is a handsome wee thing She is a lovesome wee thing, This dear wee Ruth'o mine Good luck and good health to you.

—Jimmy

On December 30, the Jacobsens were notified that Lieutenant Jimmy had been killed in service.

The war was finally over for the world, but not for the Jacobsen. Years in hiding had affected Paula and Walter so deeply, like many Holocaust survivors; it was hard for them to readjust. Post Holocaust trauma was not fully recognized until years later by society. Walter was on the road as an assistant salesman, away from home often, and even when home he hung out at the local bar. Paula became severely depressed and they had to hire a housemaid named Roosje. Teenage Ruth was responsible to take her mother to doctors and psychiatrists for treatment and medication. Paula was sinking further into depression. She was again in hiding, this time from her uncontrollable post Holocaust traumatic stress disorder (PTSD). Having already lost two childhoods, Ruth was now losing her adolescence, still a victim of the Holocaust.

Ruth attended the local Catholic High School, but had a very limited social life due to the home situation. Sister Calasanta offered to tutor her further in English and the nun became her much needed mentor. The sensitive nun saw how Ruth struggled with how terrifying it was to be a Jew. But a very moral and ethical Sister Calasanta would say to Ruth, "try to be a good Jew." Ruth promised her mother to remember her Jewish roots. Tragically, Walter and the housemaid Roosje developed a relationship as Paula's condition worsened and their marriage dissolved ending in divorce.

In 1949, Ruth and Paula applied for visas to America, but there was a long wait for entry. Due to the financial situation, although divorced, the Jacobsens all continued living in the same house. Ruth despised Roosje and gave her father an ultimatum, Roosje leaves or I do. True to her word, Ruth moved out. She graduated high school at age seventeen and found a job with room and board as a counselor in a children's residential home. Paula moved in with Tante Marie and Pa Jansen, one of the Dutch Resistor couples who hid Paula and Walter during the Holocaust.

While working at the children's home on May 17, 1952, a policeman approached Ruth. He needed her to identify her mother's body at the morgue. Shock and grief was replaced by the overwhelming sadness of realizing her mother survived the horrors of the Holocaust to be found alone and dead ten years later. Paula had taken a bus to the village pond. There was no funeral service as the Jewish faith does not provide those who commit suicide with rituals. Ruth was prohibited from attending her mother's burial, even though she did not follow the Jewish religion. Sister Calasanta provided the spiritual comfort Ruth needed to mourn her mother.

Ruth no longer had a reason to remain in Holland. On January 17, 1953 she set sail from Rotterdam to America, from the restored port the Jacobsens tried to escape from 13 years earlier. Ten days later, Ruth's first glimpse of America was the giant Ferris wheel in Coney Island. She was met in Hoboken, New Jersey by a cousin who took her to her Aunt and Uncle's apartment in New York City. Tante (aunt) Hannah, her mother's sister who she had not seen since age five, observed a Jewish traditional kosher lifestyle, which was unknown to the young secular Catholic educated Ruth. Their relationship was strained. Ruth began working at a factory to be able to move out and attended night school for typing also. She occasionally received letters from her father, but had little to say to him considering their bitter departure.

In April 1954 Ruth received a strange letter from her father, it was not written in his normal tone. He expressed that he was at peace knowing even though they were far apart; he knew she would be successful in life. He also wrote that his financial debt was insurmountable and he would be selling everything, but would give his wedding ring to Roosje to save for Ruth. Walter Jacobsen committed suicide on April 23, 1954 another victim of the Holocaust sixteen years after Kristallnacht began his nightmare.

While working as a typist in New York City Ruth attended art school. An art teacher friend helped her to develop her portfolio. The once silent and stoic hidden child survivor was shouting through her art work. This portfolio got her an exciting temporary job as a window display designer for a major department store. When the position ended, she decided to travel by bus throughout the United States to see her adopted new country. Upon return she started working as a novice in the textile industry, while privately developing her art work.

The movies are an escape for many. Fond memories of going to the movies with Lieutenant Jimmy remain with Ruth to this day. Perhaps that is why she left the textile industry after 18 years and became the first female union motion picture projectionist. She held this position for 25 years, while still developing her art.

Ruth remained in touch for many years with two of her heroes, Sister Calasanta and Cees Van Bart. Although often preferring to not speak of the war, Cees shared his experience. He was forced to work in a labor camp making airplanes for the Nazis. He was still very much an active part of the resistance. With the help of others he would try to sabotage the aircrafts. When discovered the Nazis shot several workers, beating others including Cees. Cees escaped the camp and now it was his turn to hide. He continued to help Jews even though he himself was being hunted. He was glad Ruth contacted him. Cees worried who had survived.

When Ruth Jacobsen retired at the age of sixty-three, she had achieved all of the goals she set for herself. She finally had endless time to dedicate to her art. Throughout her life she sought therapy for her experiences, especially those in her childhood, but none compared to the catharsis experienced through her expressive art. The medium of collage with images of broken headed dolls were common themes, but she lacked understanding why this was a repeated theme. Then after locating a PTSD therapist in Long Island, NY, Ruth realized she not only lost her parents, but also Ellen, her doll, was a Holocaust victim. Ellen, whose head had been glued back together after a fall, had been safe throughout the war with Tante Marie and was returned to Ruth.

Fred Lessing and Bear survived the Holocaust in hiding in Delft, Holland. Dr.Lessing is a Psychologist and fully understands the importance of dolls for the well being of children. Bear has traveled the world as part of an Anti-Defamation League (ADL) exhibit.

The Frank family was hidden from 1942-1944 by brave, righteous colleagues in the Achterhuis, the hidden back house attic. Victor Kugler, Johannes Kleiman, Miep Gies, Jan Geis, and Bep Voskuijl were the only employees who knew of the people in hiding above them. The Franks and five others were arrested by the police and Nazi SS Gestapo after a tip by an unknown informer. Entrusted heroic Miep Gies later found and saved Anne's dairy and writings and presented it to Otto Frank after his recovery from Auschwitz.

Approximately 1.5 million Jewish children were murdered during the Holocaust. Margo & Anne Frank were among them when they died of Typhus in March 1945 at Bergen-Belsen, less than a month before the concentration camp was liberated by the British. There is a memorial for Margot and Anne at the camp. There is also an Anne Frank memorial statue outside the Westerkerk Protestant Church. The diarist could see the church clock tower and wrote of the comfort the ringing bells brought her. Edith & Otto Frank were sent to the Auschwitz extermination camp, only Otto survived. Mr. Frank formed the Anne Frank Foundation to preserve the memory of his family and the writings of his diarist daughter. The original house and an attached museum is one of the most visited sites in Amsterdam. Het Achterhuis (1947, Dutch) and subsequent printings of *The Diary of a Young Girl* by Anne Frank is one of the most widely read books in history.

The remains of four Nazi destroyed synagogues in Amsterdam, dated as early as 1620 were used to construct the Joods Historisch Museum. The Portuguese Synagogue (Esnoga) of 1665 is currently undergoing renovation but was not destroyed.

Sinai Centrum, a Dutch Jewish Psychiatric Hospital opened in 1960 with the full support of the Dutch Royal Family. Its main focus was to treat Holocaust survivors suffering from PTSD. Its work with those coping with any violent trauma, especially abuse, war, and genocide continues for all people of the Netherlands.

Ruth Jacobsen is a celebrated artist and author in New York. She continues to create collages with photographs, many of which appear in her inspiring book *Rescued Images, Memories of a Childhood in Hiding* (2001.) Summarized information from Ms. Jacobsen's book appears in this chapter. Ruth's recent works include large wall murals of driftwood, sand, and paint. One such gorgeous mural appears in a Unitarian Church on Long Island, NY where she and her partner Chris are members.

A photograph of the beautiful Slot Zuylen Castle Museum and former home of Baron and Baroness Van Tuyll Van Serooskerken appears in this book. I remain grateful to Dr. Lucile Baroness Van Tuyll, granddaughter of the Baron, for the coffee and conversation overlooking the castle moat on May 29, 2010. Virtue defeats vice! Deugd Nederlagen Vice!

*Chapter Eight*

# Exodus from Budapest: Surviving Religious and Political Persecutions . . . Five Times

In April 2007 I was a keynote speaker for the Lake County Holocaust Remembrance, in Central Florida. As was the case in many of the stories in my book, either an audience member or a friend of a friend will approach me after my presentation to tell me their personal stories. I noticed one woman left early before I completed speaking for the night. She seemed overwhelmed by the subject and the photos in my power-point. I was concerned and inquired of others about this lovely lady. The next day I called Katherine to talk. Her story was captivating. But it was only when we sat privately for hours looking at her family photographs did the importance of her story hit us both.

Katherine, within a short time of our interview, had become Katalin again. She was that little three year old girl in Budapest, Hungary. Her perspective on her grandmother during the *collection action* speaks to the naivety and innocence of a child during the most horrific period of Hungarian Jewish history. Katalin's mother, Olga, was *collected*, taken off the street in front of their apartment house during the Holocaust. I had never heard of the phrase *collected* in relation to human beings before. But we now know that the Nazis did not consider Jews as even the same species, so it was easy to refer to numbers being collected so dispassionately. But wait, if Olga was taken away with the women of Budapest, how would Katalin and her brother Laszlo, age seven, survive on their own? Katalin proceeded to tell me her grandmother was sick in the bathroom. I leaned toward my new friend and asked her if grandma could have been hiding in the bathroom, not really ill, in order to survive and care for the children. There are no words to adequately describe the well of emotion and enlightenment that resulted from my simple question. Both Katalin and I were now sobbing. All those years of an innocent, childhood memory of a traumatic event gained a totally new awareness.

The original title of my book was, *Connecting with the Holocaust; Stories of Our Family's Intelligence, Courage, & Survival.* This title evolved as a result of my interview with Katalin. You will understand this significance as you read Katalin's story, some in her own words.

The Pearl of the Danube was once a favorite weekend resort for the elite of Europe. Unified Budapest was created in 1873 from the 12th century Medieval towns of Buda, "High," Pest, "Flat," and Obuda, "Old Buda." Jews in Obuda were known as merchants of fine linens and silverware. Budapest today has a Jewish population of 80,000 out of two million people.

District VII is the historic Jewish Quarter containing several synagogues, kosher bakeries, pastry and coffee shops, restaurants and hotels. One recurring architectural theme is the presence of long, inter-connected courtyards that link two parallel streets. A famous landmark, the Dohàny Street Synagogue was built in 1859 when there were 30,000 Jews living in Budapest.

The Romans were the first to discover thermal springs under the city in the first century. Some are still used in spas today. Roman architecture is still being uncovered. Sprawling country grape vines produced a lucrative viticulture industry. The Carpathian basin was later invaded by the 9th century Magyar tribe, considered the founders of the Hungarian nation. The Magyarok established small settlements, built forts, and a Royal Palace. They defended against the invading Mongols and the Turks. Sixteenth century Turkish tribes brought coffee, roses, and paprika.

In the 17th century, the Hapsburg Empire Poles occupied Hungary. Budapest continued to grow despite the many political and military upheavals. In 1849 the Chain Bridge, so called due to its chain like decorative design, opened connecting Buda and Pest. During the centuries of changing tribes and monarchies, Jews were expelled, and then invited back, under various laws and restrictions. From mid-19th through early 20th centuries, Budapest with the help of the Jewish community established schools, theaters, museums, and the metro.

By World War I Budapest was a major world capital. But the Second World War resulted in the destruction of Budapest's major buildings, bridges, and horrifically their Jewish population. There is a long history of Jewish expulsions and isolations in Europe. The Venetians in 1516 confined Jews to the ironworks or ghetto district. It is possible the word later became borghetto, or borough in Italian, and then Ghetto throughout Europe. Hitler and the architects of the Holocaust found the ghetto concept a useful tool for the final Jewish solution in Hungary. In 1938, Hungary willingly collaborated with Nazi Germany as an Axis country, and the local police became the fascist Arrow Cross militia. Approximately 200,000 Hungarian Jews were living in Budapest at that time, with an equal number living in the surrounding regions. Hungarian Prime Minister Horthy became a fascist puppet.

In 1939, thousands of Jewish men were fired from their jobs and their businesses given to non-Jewish Hungarians. Citizens like Katalin's father and maternal uncle, Miklos Landstein and Geza Levai, were among those forced into labor camps to work on the rail spurs connecting Hungary to Poland. Jews were banned from swimming in the beaches and pools preventing Olympic athletes from training and competing. Landlords and postal carriers identified the buildings where Jews resided and local police marked these buildings issuing armbands to residents with yellow stars to be worn at all times in public. Miklos was allowed to come home on a furlough, resulting a year later in the birth of Katalin. That was the last time Laszlo would see his father and Olga would see her husband. Miklos and Geza were starved, worked to death, and murdered in Kiskunhalas, 130 km (81 miles) south of Budapest, alongside the rails.

Judith Bihaly, age 10, lived in Budapest with her Catholic parents. On March 19, 1944, she became a Jew when Germany fully occupied Hungary. Records showed that she had a deceased grandparent that was Jewish. The one-quarter blood law made her a Jew. She and 400,000 eastern European Jews were deported to Auschwitz by cattle cars on the rails built by Jewish slave labor. Many others were marched by foot to the Austrian Mauthausen death camp. The Royal British Air Force contacted Churchill with surveillance information showing the additional rail spur being built from Hungary to Birkenau. Churchill contacted FDR and asked if the Allies should bomb this spur. The decision was made not to bomb. The Nazis transported 426,000 Jews from April to July 1944 to Auschwitz-Birkenau.

The Dohàny Street Synagogue became a shelter for many Jews during the harsh winter of 1944. Many died and were buried at the edge of the ghetto wall in the temple courtyard. Adolf Eichmann arrived in Budapest to personally oversee the Jewish Final Solution and the liquidation of the Budapest Ghetto. Obscenely, his office was located in the women's balcony behind the beautiful rose colored stained glass. The fascist Arrow Cross Hungarian Police and the SS Gestapo proceeded rapidly to eliminate the remaining Jews.

An "Aktion" or notice to report appeared on all the doors of the apartment building where Katalin, Laszlo, Olga, and her sister-in-law were living. From a young child's perspective, prior to the Aktion, Katalin's life was bearable, as she could play and be protected by her mother. It was harder for Laszlo as he could no longer attend school and see his friends. The next morning Olga kissed her children good-bye and descended the three story building to the street below. The Arrow Cross and the Gestapo ordered the woman into rows of four. Katalin and Laszlo followed their mother downstairs. Suddenly Laszlo ran to Olga, clinging to her waist. She kicked and pushed her son away, telling him to take his sister upstairs. Laszlo was so angry at his mother for leaving him, but her actions, although harsh in the eyes of a seven year old boy, actually saved his life, as the police were about to shoot him. Olga's love must have been agonizingly painful. The women of Budapest were collected and transported to Birkenau. In the initial interview of Katalin for this book, I asked her how she and her brother survived on their own, with their father and uncle dead and their mother and aunt heading to a death camp. Very innocently, as if this 68 year old woman was a little three year old girl again, Katalin said, "Oh Grandma had a tummy ache and was in the toilet closet." An intelligent and courageous survival plan by Olga and her mother allowed the hidden Grandmother to remain and care for Katalin, Laszlo, and their two cousins.

By September 5, 1945, after the Soviets liberated Hungary, Katalin, Laszlo, their two cousins, and Grandmother were among the Jews still alive in Budapest. Fifty percent of the Jewish population had been murdered. Looking out the window on this date, young Katalin saw what looked like two ghosts walking toward her apartment. They were so thin and pale she could not recognize them. Stopping where they were collected the year before, Olga and her sister-in-law looked up. Katalin and grandma screamed and cried; they had returned; they had survived.

Olga Landstein was back but it did not feel like Budapest was her home anymore. She felt the only safe place on the planet was Eretz Israel, the land of Israel, the eternal homeland of Judaism. Jews had assimilated throughout Europe and the Russian territories, but under Hitler's Holocaust, many in the Zionist movement realized they needed their own country. Since most of the world turned blind and deaf to the requests for rescue from desperate Jews, a Jewish country that would never say no to Jewish refugees ever again was needed.

The Zionists in Hungary and throughout Europe established agricultural and educational camps for orphaned Jewish Children. Working covertly with the Haganah Jewish Defense and Resistance fighters, their goal was to smuggle the children past the British blockade into Palestine. Olga joined the Zionist organization and was hired as a camp counselor to the orphaned children. Two of the orphaned children were Laszlo and Katalin.

They had to pretend that Olga was not their mother in order to stay in this program. Young Katalin saw this as "play acting," and being a half orphan it wasn't a big lie. This was painful as a mother for Olga, but a way to offer a better life for her children. The children adjusted well to Kibbutz camp life in the northern countryside outside Budapest. Later the entire camp was transported to Austria for several months during which Jewish war orphans of many countries joined them. The camp was growing in numbers, the official language was Hebrew, the songs, the studies and military training disguised as games were preparing the youngsters for a self-sufficient, independent lifestyle.

*Katalin & Laszlo Landstein Budapest.*
*Courtesy of Katherine Landstein Mitchell.*

When it was time for mobilization of the kibbutz camp, the children were hidden in potato sacks on the backs of covered trucks and were told they must be very still, not even a cough. After many hours they arrived in a port in Marseilles, to board a rickety old ship with two signs on its side: "Haganah" and "EXODUS." The Exodus was purchased by Mossad, Israeli Intelligence, from the United States. The ship was originally the USS Warfield, which had been decommissioned by the Navy in 1928, then briefly used as a boat in Virginia on the Chesapeake Bay. On July 11, 1947, the ship set sail from France with 4,515 adults and 655 children, Jewish Holocaust orphaned refugees Aliyah Bet, illegally emigrating to Palestine.

The Exodus was in International water, 20 nautical miles from the port of Haifa on July 20. As she raised the Zionist flag and attempted to run the British blockade, destroyers rammed the Exodus from both sides, and boarded the ship. The refugees and crew threw canned goods at the British sailors. A volunteer crewman, US Naval officer William Bernstein from California was one of several people killed during the three hour melee. The United Nations team ((UNSCOP) commissioned to recommend whether Israel should become a nation state was watching the ship from the shoreline. As the teargas cleared, they could hear the singing of Hatikvah, "Our Hope is not Lost," the Zionist anthem. A year later the British mandate of Palestine ended, establishing the declaration of the State of Israel in May 1948.


## A CHILD REMEMBERS

It was crowded and dark. The interior of the cattle ship seemed to be an endless black tunnel with moaning and groaning of invisible people. To me everything seemed big. I was only 6 years old. Everything and everyone was overwhelming. The stench of the unwashed was the norm. I knew to keep my head down, sit low in the triple-decker bunk bed and make no noise. When I had a chance to go to the porthole, I was too short to see out. Someone had to lift me up. Then I saw the big English battleship with its guns and shiny sides moving alongside our wooden vessel. I was ordered by my mother to go back to our bunk and stay with her. By now, it was OK for people to know that my brother and I had our real mother with us. Originally, when we first embarked, my brother and I were not allowed to tell anyone that we were only half orphans. Our mother had to take care of dozens of children in order for her to get a job as a supervising adult. She had to agree not to tell anyone that she had two living children in the group. Her goal was to deliver her two children to freedom; to Palestine; to the land of milk and honey. Now, after we were all piled into bunks, she had the joy of having her two kids close to her. But my brother wanted to spread his wings at age 10. He wanted to be the MAN. He gave her a hard time wanting to go on deck and fight for the cause. But his budding manhood was overruled.

The gunfight began. We heard word that some young fighters who were up top had slipped on the oily deck and fell into the deep black water. As the gunfight went on, I saw large gaping holes in the side of our ship. Teargas filled the entire space. My mother was smart enough to have wet towels for our faces and for that time even my brother settled down and let our mother doctor us to keep us alive.

The shooting battle wouldn't end. The darkness of the belly of the ship, where we were huddled together with what seemed to me to be thousands of other Jewish refugees, was getting deeper and meaner. I was not afraid because my mother had her arms around me and my brother was holding my hand. I had no reason to be afraid. I wasn't crying, but the teargas made me cough. I didn't know if I was allowed to cough because on our trip to meet the ship, I had to be silent so no one would ever know that there was a living person under the potato sacks in the big produce truck. I was one of many small children hidden under the potato sacks and told to be silent no matter what. Holding back, holding in, being silent, was the rule.

Now, with the teargas burning my face and eyes, as I was pressing the wet towel against my face, I was afraid to utter a sound. Well trained. But somehow, I wondered if anyone would hear me, since the gunfight up above was so loud. My class leader and her friends, who were at least 18, were all on deck, fighting back, trying to make the English gunboat give up and leave us alone.

The holes in our ship became larger. We were taking on water. There was the cry of Orthodox Jews davening, praying to the East, although I wasn't sure they knew where East was. That was all they could do stuck in the underbelly of this big cattle boat. Then there were sounds of unintelligible instructions over the loudspeaker, followed by silence. Word came that we had given up to the British and we had to exit the ship.

Panic set in. This was a real cattle ship. The exits were narrow, made for cattle to wind their way out of the ship. We were not cattle. Humans panic. There were dozens and dozens of people choking from teargas, trying to get out all at once. My mother held us back. Kept the wet towels on our faces and slowly guided us toward the exit. We lined up and little-by-little, by push and shove, we got into the cattle walk exit ramp moving along until we reached the outside. We breathed.

We breathed again and again. Air; Clean smell; Breathing; what a lovely thing. My mother moved us forward and hung on to my brother's hand. He had an incredible urge of wanting to be a man, although not yet 11, and wanting to lead the way, and wanting to fight. Finally, our mother pulled rank, ordering him to stay with us.

We were now on top deck. I can still see the wet, oily and slippery top deck where earlier I heard the fighting going on, or was it rather the resistance going on. I saw the ropes that were put up to keep the regular people like us, on course as we were leaving the ship named EXODUS.

Then, finally, we were on solid ground. We were on land at the Haifa dock. We couldn't walk all that easily without feeling the rumbling shaking of the ship under our feet. Before we knew it, we were directed to cross the dock and embark on the closest of one of, I think, five British gun boats.

I was a small child. The English soldiers lining the sides of the gangplank picked me up and handed me up the gangplank from one to another as if I were a piece of meat. My mother had no choice but to rush up and follow me as she was dragging my brother.

The next thing I knew we were in nice, clean, well washed, exterior bedding, all enclosed in high wire fences; Cages. We were in cages. It was outdoors, so there would be no reason for any more teargas. It was outdoors

*Exodus Ship port Haifa Palestine (eretz Israel) 1947. Courtesy of United States Holocaust Memorial Museum http://www.ushmm.org.*

although inside wire fencing. Cages. Showers, bedding, group seating, all outdoors on deck of the River Empire. In cages.

My Mother was praying for us not to be taken to Cypress. She has just escaped Auschwitz and feared the possibility of going to Cypress, another kind of concentration camp. She knew. She was not old, but she knew. She prayed and prayed, and the ship went to Hamburg, Germany. I was a child.

—M. Katalin Landstein, 2008

The British ships returned to Hamburg Germany and the refugees from the Exodus were relocated to Displaced Persons Camps in the British Allied controlled zones. The gray barracks were too much like the concentration camp Olga had just survived, so she soon would find a way out. Olga contacted her mother in Budapest. Katalin's grandmother had a friend who helped them during the Holocaust by smuggling needed food and supplies to them. A week later, Lali the well paid but trustworthy smuggler, cut a hole in the rear camp fence at night and the three Landsteins escaped the DP camp returning by train to Budapest.

Katalin had forgotten her native Hungarian and had to be tutored before starting second grade. She studied gymnastics and became an award winning national competitor. Laszlo was a mathematical genius who assimilated much quicker. Olga found a job in a food packaging company. So the family appeared to be settling back into life in the city. Although Hungary was liberated from Nazi occupation, the Russian liberators decided to stay, and Hungary was now under Soviet communist control. Russian was taught in the schools and religion was replaced by the worship of Communism. Katalin and Laszlo were entitled to certain opportunities by the government as children effected by the Holocaust. She had been awarded a full scholarship to study Fine Arts at the University and aspired to become a writer and filmmaker. Laszlo was already in the University finishing his engineering degree.

Then on October 23, 1956 a peaceful protest by college students turned violent. A bronze statue of Stalin was toppled. But freedom was short lived, as Russian tanks overran the city crushing the rebellion. Laszlo was one of the protestors. The revolution had begun. Fearing for his life, he and three friends hired a truck driver to take them across the Austrian border. He was then able to obtain a visa to the USA. The Soviets sealed the border.

Olga decided it was time to leave Budapest for good. She began selling their furniture for money to travel. Katalin wanted to stay and continue her studies, but Olga insisted they should join Laszlo in America. Katalin, now almost 16 was told to dress in layers. Olga paid a man with a horse and carriage to take them to the Russian guarded Austrian border. She bribed the soldiers with money and vodka, which they immediately imbibed, quickly becoming drunk. Mother and daughter crossed into Austria, running through the snowy forest. Olga collapsed into the snow, "I can't go any further," telling Katalin to continue to Vienna without her. The exhausted mother had delivered her two children once again to safety. Katalin now become the parent, picking her mother out of the snow and saying "I need you to help me carry these bags." On December 23, 1956, mother and daughter were found in the forest on the Austro-Hungarian border. They were safe.

Four months later, arrangements were made for Visas and a flight to the United States. Olga and Katalin boarded their flight to the US when they suddenly were forced to land in Frankfurt. A wing to the plane had caught fire. Olga survived for the fifth time! They were transported to a Boy Scout Camp overnight, which had to cause a frightening post traumatic response from Olga. The next day they were driven back to the airport for their flight to America. Their plane landed in Newark, NJ where a Red Cross Hungarian translator helped the new immigrants. They took a bus from Grand Central

Station in NYC to Toledo, Ohio, where Olga, Laszlo, and Katalin were reunited as a family on Katalin's sixteenth birthday.

Approximately 100,000 Jews were saved by Raoul Wallenberg & Carl Lutz, Swedish Diplomats who issued Protective Papers from 1943-1945. They personally financed Swedish safe zone housing for victims. Wallenberg angered the Hungarian Arrow Cross when he pulled people off transports handing out protective Swiss passes right on the train platforms. On Jan.17, 1945 Wallenberg disappeared after attending a meeting to insure that the safety of the Jews of Budapest would be honored after he returned to his country. It is unknown if he was murdered by the Arrow Cross, or has been claimed, was taken into custody by a Soviet escort to Siberia, where he died in prison, falsely charged with espionage. Memorials and statues to Diplomats Lutz and Wallenberg can be seen throughout Budapest.

In 1989 communism collapsed along with the statue of Lenin, making Hungary a democracy. The Dohany synagogue has been restored to its magnificence. It is heavily guarded by security. Lucy Braun, an orphaned child Holocaust survivor, was adopted by the synagogue members after the war. She sells her beautiful hand crafted challah bread covers and wedding glass bags in a kiosk right outside the entrance to the synagogue.

Sculptor Gyula Pauer and poet Can Togay created the *Shoes on the Danube Promenade* (2005) Memorial to the victims from 1944-1945 of the Arrow Cross Militiamen. The Iron shoes represent the shoes Jews had to leave behind for their murderers, as they were shot and fell into the Danube River. The memorial is on the Pest side river bank near the Parliament.

Judith Bihaly survived Auschwitz and was told simply and cruely to go home. Asking questions along the way she found her childhood apartment. "I am Judth Bihaly," she said. "If you don't get away from here right now I'm going to let the dogs lose on you," said the person at the door. She left and checked into a Zionist home for orphans. In 1947, Eleanor Roosevelt convinced President Harry Truman to expand the US immigration quotas to Holocaust survivors, something her husband refused to do as President. Judith was one of one million surviving refugees taken in by 113 countries from 1945-1950.

After Laszlo graduated college and Katalin graduated High School, the Landstein's moved to NYC. Olga became very good in her job as a seamstress. Laszlo completed his graduate degree in Mechanical Engineering at Columbia University, is married and lives in NY. Katalin had a gymnastic scholarship to study Physical Education at Hunter Teachers College, but had to manage the family responsibilities. To channel her frustrations she began writing and her one act play was performed off Broadway. She met her first husband, an actor and they moved to Hollywood, California. Katalin became a screen writer for television and motion pictures. She is a member of the Writers Guild of America, has remarried, and lives in Florida.

Olga lived to see the birth of three grandchildren from her son and daughter. Sadly, shortly after the birth of Katalin's daughter, Olga became very sick. She had repeated gynecological problems and infections. The infections affected her teeth, her heart, and finally her liver. It is possible that in 1944, as a beautiful, young Hungarian woman, Olga was assigned to the gynecological medical building where the Nazi doctors at Auschwitz performed horrific experiments. Although a five time survivor of several traumas and escapes, in 1969, at age 59, Olga died of post traumatic medical complications 25 years after the Holocaust.

Katalin and Laszlo met in 2009 in Florida for a loving reunion in their mother's memory.

## Chapter Nine

# The Boy in the Suitcase:
# Sosua Dominican Republic

Why would one dictator welcome Jewish refugees, while another evil dictator was determined to exterminate all Jews? This question gnawed in my head. I had no intention of adding another chapter to my book. But the story would not go away and compelled me to learn more. The result is a fascinating journey in 2009 to the remote town of Sosua in the Dominican Republic, and to the not so distant city of Englewood Cliffs in New Jersey, USA.

General Trujillo, president of the country of the Dominican Republic ruled his island with fear and cruelty. Trujillo was charming towards those who revered him, and dangerous to those who opposed him. Rumors reached the outside international community of killings of his own people. The League of Nations was beginning to investigate stories of genocide committed by Trujillo's army against people from the bordering country of Haiti. Three-quarters of the Island of Hispaniola is occupied by the Dominican Republic, with the other quarter of the Island being the country of Haiti. Approximately 18,000 Haitians who were living within the Dominican border were murdered by the Army in 1937.

On a distant continent, world leaders were meeting in Évian-les-Bains, France. The 1938 Evian Conference, as it became known was initiated by the United States President Franklin D. Roosevelt. He chose to send a low ranking government official instead of attending himself. This move suspiciously appears as though FDR was protecting his political career against an antisemitic congress. Wealthy industrialists like Henry Ford were helping Germany and also financially backing FDR. The question of large numbers of Jewish citizens trying to leave Germany and Austria due to the escalating harsh conditions instituted under the 1935 Nuremberg laws was the focus of this conference. Incredulously almost all 32 countries with representatives in attendance refused to increase their immigration quotas. Australia offered to issue 15,000 immediate visas. The Dominican Republic stunned the delegates offering to issue up to 100,000 temporary refugee status visas.

Virgilio Trujillo Molina, brother of President Rafael Trujillo, represented the Dominican Republic at the Evian Conference. In 1940 Trujillo reached an agreement with the United States and the League of Nations to issue Visas to German and Austrian Jews. Cecelia Razovsky Assistant Executive Director of the US National Refugee Service arranged for ships, paid for by Jewish aid organizations in America, such as the American Jewish Joint Distribution Committee (JDC) to transport fleeing refugees from Germany to the Dominican Republic. The Dominican Republic Settlement Association, DORSA, a subsidiary of JDC began renovation of an abandoned banana plantation in the northern Dominican village of Sosua. On May 10, 1940 Trujillo welcomed the arrival of the former Italian ship Conte Biancamano, now the USS Hermitage, to the northern Dominican region of Puerto Plata. On this ship was the Boy in the Suitcase.

In 1492 in Spain, Jewish bankers helped finance the voyage of Christopher Columbus. Shortly after he set sail for the Americas, under pressure from the Catholic Church, Sephardic Jews were told to convert or risk being killed. The Spanish Inquisition brought the first Jewish immigrants to the Island of Hispaniola in 1492. Bartholomew Columbus, a cartographer, followed his brother to the Caribbean Island and named the southern capital Santo Domingo in 1496. Jewish doctors, merchants, sailors, and clergy continued to sail from Spain to this new land. As they had done in Spain, many Jews assimilated into society, hiding their Jewish identity. Centuries later this island would once again offer a haven from religious persecution for Jews. Ashkenazi Jewish immigrants arrived from Nazi Germany and Austria in 1940. They restored and settled the land in Sosua, on the northern part of the island, east of Puerto Plata.

Jewish organizations in America were pressuring Roosevelt to change the immigration quota to allow persecuted refugees to flee Europe and enter the United States. Jewish organizations, such as The American Jewish Joint Distribution Committee (JDC) offered to pay for the visas of fleeing Jews. In 1939, at a State Department cocktail party, Roosevelt was speaking to his Commissioner of Immigration James Houghteling about the proposed Wagner-Rogers Bill. This bill by New York Democratic Senator Robert F. Wagner, a German American, and Massachusetts Democratic Representative Edith Nourse Rogers would have allowed for the issuance of 20,000 emergency visas for Jewish children to enter the United States from Germany. Political leaders and industrialists like Senator Robert Reynolds of North Carolina and Henry Ford with ties to American and German Nazis attached amendments to anchor the bill. Strong antisemitism in Congress and the public, and a policy of isolationism following the depression all added to the fervor against the bill. Mrs. Eleanor Roosevelt turned to Mrs. Laura Houghteling and asked her opinion of the Wagner-Rogers Bill. "The problem with this bill is "that 20,000 ugly [Jewish] children will all too soon grow up into 20,000 ugly adults." Laura Delano Houghteling was the cousin of FDR. Roosevelt allowed the bill to die, along with 10,000 Jewish children that spring. Realizing the U.S. failure to act, the British saved approximately 7,000 Children in the Kindertransport from Germany to the U.K.

The Evian International Conference on the status of Jewish Refugees took place at the beautiful Evian-Les-Bains tourist resort on Lake Geneva, France, on July 6, 1938. The refusal of 30 countries to relax their immigration quotas sent a strong message to Hitler and Himmler. The message was that the world will be a bystander as Germany makes all of Europe *Frei von Juden.*

Virgilio Trujillo Molina, General Trujillo's brother, who was representing the Dominican Republic in the Evian conference, surprised everybody when he announced that the Dominican Republic would grant 100,000 temporary immigrant visas. He also stated that the Jews and their descendents would be protected from religious persecution. There were conditions and motives to this generous offer. The new emigrants had to agree to learn Spanish, learn to be farmers and pay back the government for the land, pay their own ship passage, and consider marrying local Dominicans. General Trujillo was being investigated for the Haitian Genocide by the League of Nations. By rescuing Jews he felt he could improve his humanitarian image. Trujillo also saw an opportunity for well educated, fair skinned young European adults to develop the abandoned northern region of the country and lighten the Dominican skin tones through intermarriage. According to local Sosuan legend, Trujillo already had a favorable impression of Jews. His daughter Flora de Oro was studying in Paris and had difficulty making friends. One girl, Lucy Cahn understood discrimination very well. She became Flora's roommate and dear friend. After Lucy's traditional Jewish wedding, she and her husband honeymooned on their Dominican plantation which was a generous gift from Papa Trujillo.

Why does the country want these settlers? Because the dictator Trujillo wants a white country, and interestingly, Jews are seen as white—Ironically, the bitter race prejudice in the little Caribbean republic creates a haven for victims of a different race prejudice in the Reich. Jews are white, they are Europeans; they will bring energy and higher standards of life and better ways of doing things. They will mingle eventually with the population, increasing the precious proportion of white blood. Also they bring money. It'll give them political clout as the country that took refugees. ("Caribbean Refuge" 1940)

In January of 1939, the American Jewish Joint Distribution Committee (JDC) went to the Dominican Republic to make the offer official. The United

States delegation consisted of Dr. Joseph Rosen, an expert of agricultural farming. What they saw was an abandoned Banana Plantation with running water, electricity, and some former worker cabins. Dr. Rosen saw potential in this location as a sanctuary for escaping Jews. The Joint Distribution Committee hired New York attorney James Rosenberg as head of the Dominican Republic Settlement Association (DORSA) which purchased 26,000 acres in Sosua. Each settler was given 80 acres, 10 cows, 1 bull, 1 mule, and 1 horse. The immigrants had to pay back the government for the land and assets at the charge of 20 Pesos per month. It should be noted that originally the plan called for a 99 year lease, which was rejected by the cooperative.

> Article 1: The Republic, in accordance with its Constitution and Laws, hereby, by means of this Accord, guarantees the Settlers and their descendents the opportunity to continue their lives and their occupations free from interferences, discrimination or persecution, with rights of freedom of religion and religious ceremonies, with equal civil, legal and economic rights, as well as all other rights inherent to Human beings. (DORSA & Dominican Govt. 1939)

The first group of Jewish refugees from Nazi Germany arrived in Sosua on May 10, 1940. There were to be only adults, but unexpectedly, arrived 26 men, 10 women, and one baby boy. The JDC hired a multilingual educator to teach the new immigrants Spanish and to facilitate their adjustment in a new land. His name was Mr. Louis Hess.

The Hess family lived in the medieval town of Erfurt, Germany. The 1933 antisemitic Nuremberg laws prohibited Jews from owning businesses. The Hess family shoe factory became government controlled. Louis' father told him to leave the country immediately. He was able to get a tourist visa and went to Spain and his parents went to France, then to the United States.

While living in Spain Louis, now Luis became fluent in Spanish, adding to his other languages of German, Hebrew and English. He applied for a position in the Dominican Republic Embassy. The Ambassador gave him a free visa to go to Ciudad Trujillo (Santo Domingo) to help with translations for the expected wave of new immigrants. DORSA paid his salary and relocated him from the Capital City to Sosua.

Rudolf and Ilse Loewenthal Herzberg had a comfortable life in Berlin, Germany, under the democratic Weimar Republic. Rudolf was a successful lawyer and Ilse worked in a haberdashery. The ascent to power of the National Socialist Party and the declaration in 1933 of Hitler as Chancellor changed life forever for this typical, well educated, upper middle class Jewish couple. On the evenings of Nov. 9-10, 1938 Jewish owned businesses were smashed, throwing shattered glass and lives throughout the streets of Berlin and surrounding towns. Synagogues were set ablaze and destroyed. Following

Kristallnacht, the Herzberg's knew they had to leave their homeland. There was a poster from a Jewish American organization on a street pole in 1939 inviting Jews to apply for visas to the Dominican Republic. They applied for two of the precious visas to Sosua, a land they knew little about, except that they would accept Jewish refugees. The Herzbergs continued commuting to work in Berlin, now forced to wear yellow stars on their coats. Ilse was seated on her usual commuter bus when a Nazi soldier boarded and asked for her seat. She refused stating she was pregnant. The Nazi slapped her hard across the face, knocking her out of her seat.

Two Herzberg visas were granted in 1940, but by then their infant son, Denny had been born. The family packed two suitcases, including some strong, narcotic cough medicine Ilse's sister, a pediatrician had given them for the baby in case he got sick on the ship. They took the train from Berlin to the port in Genoa, Italy. As Rudolf and Ilse arrived at the pier, the Gestapo shouted *"zwei visas"* and grabbed baby Denny from his mother's arms. Rudolph instinctively lunged for his son, telling the guard that he would leave the baby with his sister-in-law and they would return shortly. They had heard the horror stories from Warsaw Poland of attempts to smuggle babies out of the ghetto. Nazi soldiers would throw the discovered babies into the air and shoot them for sport. The parents had to take a chance.

Rudolf & Ilse went behind a vacant building at the dock. Ilse emptied the clothes from one of the suitcases. Rudy found a sharp rock to use to punch holes in its side for air. They drugged baby Denny and placed him inside the luggage. On April 10, 1940 the Herzberg family boarded the decommissioned Italian vessel Conte Biancamano, now known as the USS Hermitage, and set sail for the Dominican Republic.

Once safely in international waters the suitcase was opened and baby Denny and his parents began their new lives. The journey took four long weeks. Their quarters were in steerage and they had limited water and mainly potatoes to eat. By the time they reached the Dominican Republic, baby Denny was suffering from malnutrition. On May 10, upon arrival in Puerto Plata Denny's first clean clothing was a dress, since all his clothes were left behind.

He was hospitalized and required almost a year of medical treatment. As a result, his speech was severely delayed. Finally at age four, the boy in the suitcase was speaking German and Spanish fluently. Ilse's sister heroically remained in Germany medically treating Jews. Right before her scheduled deportation to Auschwitz she fatally injected herself.

Adolf Eichmann was receiving money from an attorney in Austria to stamp visas for exiting Jews going to Palestine. Himmler told Eichmann if he wants to keep his head and his job, he needed to shut down this operation

*Baby Denny & Mom Sosua, Dominican Republic. Courtesy of Denny Herzberg.*

immediately. Heydrich in 1941 informed Eichmann of the master plan for ex- termination of the Jews. January 1942 the three would all attend the Wannsee Conference outlining the Final Solution to the Jewish Problem. Erich Benja- min was sent to Buchenwald. Ruth Echt was given a visa, but her ship went to Shanghai China. Kurt Wellisch received the very last visa, catching the very last train to the very last ship leaving for Sosua on December 7, 1941. Only an estimated 800 visas were officially issued.

Mr. Hess created the first trilingual school on the Island, which was later named in his honor. In the evening he taught adults, in the daytime it was an elementary and middle school for grades K-8. Both Dominican and Jewish holidays were celebrated. The grateful adults and children who were rescued by Trujillo paraded before the dictator in their white cotton uniforms. Keep- ing with the promise of assimilating into the Dominican culture, Jewish men like Luis attended local dances. It was while dancing the Meringue that he fell in love and married Ana Julia de Silva. They had two sons, two grand- children, and a great grandchild. Ana and Luis practiced the Jewish religion as well as maintaining the Dominican heritage.

One of the first structures to be built in Sosua in 1940 was the synagogue, keeping with the dictator's promise of religious freedom. Denny Herzberg, Rene Kirchheimmer, Benny Katz, Freddy Milz, and Joe Benjamin, sons of settlers had their Bar Mitvas at age 13 in this synagoga. The entire community of Sosua attended the first Passover Seder celebration. The Dominican cooks were taught how to prepare Jewish meals and attended the annual communal event. The first Rosh Hashanah, the Jewish New Year in the Synagoga was attended by President Trujillo in September 1941. He briefly spoke to the congregation wishing them in Hebrew "L'Shona Tova!"

Single and family barrack style housing was built by the settlers with the help of DORSA experts. The first Jewish cemetery was also needed shortly after their arrival. Many settlers, who never saw a horse, now loved riding them as transportation and sport. Jewish doctors and dentists opened a medical clinic and took care of local Dominicans for free as a thank you for the Dominican hospitality. Café House was the entertainment pavilion for theater products, opera, movies, music, and joke telling comedy acts. "So we stared at the cows. What happens next? Does one get hold of the tail and pump and somehow milk comes out?" Edith Gersten "It was all very difficult-The language, the climate, social situations-but we were saved." Ruth Kohn, Sosua Exhibit, Museum of Jewish Heritage, NY 2008.

The Jews will bloom where they are planted, said a representative of the JDC. The greatest evidence of this is in the highly successful Dairy Farms and Factories created by the Jewish Sosuan Cooperative. Productos Sosua to this day is a major producer of excellent cheese and sausage. In 2004 the company was sold, but the offspring of the settlers remain shareholders.

After the war, many settlers left the country for several reasons. Some had trouble adjusting to the heat. Other wanted to live in larger Jewish communities. The young people especially wanted to attend universities that provided more advanced degrees and careers. By 1956 Sosuans realized that political change was coming. Fear of a revolution led the original settlers to send their second generation teenagers and young adults, born in Dominican Republic, to live with relatives in America. Rene Kirchheimer, whose father Arthur, renamed Arturo was one of the original Sosuan pioneers, went to study in New York. In 1958 President Trujillo conferred full citizen status to the original Jewish immigrants of Sosua. Three years later he was assassinated and in 1961 Democracy came to the Republic. Regardless of the politics, the Sosuan Jews remained loyal, grateful citizens. Their unconditional acceptance by the Dominican people is repeatedly and strongly expressed by the Jews of Sosua.

In the Jewish cemetery where original settler Lutbert, father of Fanny Consuelo Wachsmann is buried, evidence of the joining of the Dominican and the Jewish communities can most dramatically be seen. On the headstones are written epitaphs in both German and Spanish honoring the original settlers and their spouses.

There are approximately 300 Jews in the Dominican Republic, mainly in the capital of Santo Domingo. Many have intermarried and continue to practice Judaism, especially on the Holidays. Three synagogues remain in the Republic, two in the capital and the original one in Sosua. An itinerant Rabbi conducts monthly services in the Sosuan synagogue upon request. In 1990 on the 50th anniversary of Jewish Sosua, the Museo Judío de Sosúa opened. This unique museum shares the grounds with the Synogoga. The curator of the Museo Judio is Ivonne Strauss Milz, native Sosuan daughter of settlers Herman and Heidi Strauss. Her husband Freddy is a second generation settler's son. They have two children.

Kurt Wellisch escaped from Austria with a visa to Sosua. He was forced to leave school, denied an education under the antisemitic Nazi decrees. In 2005 Juli Wellisch de Moncada, a University professor in Santo Domingo, and her family were invited to the school in Vienna to receive her father's diploma and apology from the Austrian government.

Fanny Consuelo Wachsmann, daughter of Lutbert and Blascena Gonzalez lives in Sosua and is an administrator for the cooperative. Above her office door is a traditional Jewish mezuzah. Born and married in Sosua, she has two daughters.

Joe Benjamin considers himself a "Jewminican." Joe was born in Shanghai China while his parents were waiting to emigrate to Sosua. His father escaped from the Buchenwald concentration camp. Raised in Sosua, he is an engineer who studied in Pennsylvania, but returned to redesign the Dairy factory. He has two interracial adopted children. When asked about Trujillo the dictator, Joe shared: "It was not for us to judge Trujillo; we could only judge our relationship as Jews with Trujillo. We were never rejected, we were always accepted."

Ruth Echt also made her way from Shanghai to Sosua, marrying Werner Myerstein who had emigrated from Germany to Sosua. Ruth lives in Miami and Sosua and has two daughters, Evelyn and Hedy, and two grandchildren. One of the 5,000 visas that were later found unprocessed in a desk drawer of a United States immigration officer would have allowed Ruth direct transport to Sosua in 1941.

I had the great historic honor of meeting Mr. Luis Hess on July 20, 2009. He was still a brilliant sincere man at age 100. His school and the hundreds of Sosuans he educated and helped is his legacy. He and his wife Ana Julia had two sons, grandchildren, and great-grandchildren. Mr. Hess died at age 101 and is buried with his beloved wife in the Jewish cemetery in Sosua.

Baby Denny is a successful international businessman in Englewood Cliffs, New Jersey. Mr. Herzberg studied in Germany and the U.S., obtaining his Masters in Business Administration at the University of Illinois in 1965. He is fluent in Hebrew, German, English, and Spanish. He and his wife, children and grandchildren return to Sosua annually. Mr. Herzberg generously gives back to the community in many ways, but one action is very significant. He works with impoverished countries that have contaminated water to make potable drinking water for their citizens. Denny has a ritual every Friday at the end of the work week. His employees join him for a wine toast of thanks and to life, *L'Chaim!*

Approximately 25 Jewish families live and work permanently in Sosua. The second and now third generation adult children of the settlers continue to manage the cooperative established by their settler parents. The Dairy factory and original lands continue to generate income for them. Those that live out of the country return for annual business meetings, reunions, and family vacations. They remain in contact with each other and are a very close, generous, grateful community to this day. "Sosua, a community born of pain and nurtured in love must, in the final analysis represent the ultimate triumph of life." "Sosúa, una comunidad que nace del dolor y criado en el amor debe, en última instancia, representan el triunfo último de la vida" (*Museo* Judío de *Sosúa 2009).*

*Chapter Ten*

# We Are Here!

*Needle sisters Sheryl & Susanne. Courtesy of snc.*

*Raquel (Gershgorn) Gordon. Courtesy of R.Gordon.*

*Gale Benczman Sussman. Courtesy of Harold Fowler wolfcreekphotography.com.*

*Silberstein sisters Shirley & Phyllis. Courtesy of Shirley Schuman.*

*Pierre Haskelson. Courtesy of Pierre Haskelson.*

Jose Loeb. Courtesy of snc.

Marcelle (Micke) Destrain Gimborn.
Courtesy of Micke Gimborn.

*Ruth Jacobsen. Courtesy of Susanne Needle.*

*Katalin & Laszlo Landstein. Courtesy of Katherine Mitchell.*

*Denny Herzberg. Courtesy of snc.*

# Author's Disclaimer

I hope my book has brought new insight to you about the Holocaust from a very personal perspective. The stories told to me and the subsequent research of the history in the shtetls, villages, cities, and countries of our families are all real. The genre of this book is narrative non-fiction. I am telling you stories which are all based in truth and enhanced by historical fact. However, if in the recollection of events during such a traumatic time, myself, or the survivor, or the family member sharing their story may unintentionally provide information that is inaccurate. You are welcome to contact me with academic reference citations that will allow me to correct any inaccuracies for subsequent publication.

# Bibliography

Abramowicz, M., & Hoffenberg, E. (Directors). *As If It Were Yesterday*. (Available from the National Center for Jewish Film, Brandeis University, Lown 102, MS053, Waltham MA 02454). 1980. Dvd.

Abramowitz, Mayer. "The View From 82: The Cold War in Berlin's DP Camps." http://www.jewishfederations.org/page.aspx?id=79327. Retrieved 06-04-11.

Agosín, M. *Memory, Oblivion, and Jewish Culture In Latin America*, University of Texas Press 2005.

Arad, Y. *Ghetto in Flames: The Struggle and Destruction of the Jews in Vilna in the Holocaust*. Jerusalem: Yad Vashem Martyrs' and Heroes' Remembrance Authority. 1980.

Arad, Y., Krakowski, S., & Spector, S. *The Einsatzgruppen Reports: Selections from the Dispatches of the Nazi Death Squads' Campaign Against the Jews July 1941-1943*. New York: Holocaust Library. 1989.

Auquier, A. *Souvenirs De Guerre Et Liberation De Quaregnon Et D'Ailleurs*. Belgium: Quaregnon, 1994.

Auschwitz. *United States Holocaust Memorial Museum*. Retrieved from http://www.ushmm.org/wlc/en/article.php?ModuleId=10005189. 1 April 2010.

Avital, Z., Dabrowska, D., Wein, A., Weiss, A., & Jakubowicz, A. Eastern Galicia. In *Encyclopedia of Jewish Communities, Poland* (Vol. 2). Jerusalem: Yad Vashem. 1980.

Baranova, O. Nationalism, anti-Bolshevism, or the will to survive? Collaboration in Belarus under the Nazi occupation 1941-1944. *European Review of History, 15(2)* 113. 2008.

Barroso, M. (Director). *In the Time of the Butterflies*. (Available from MGM Home Entertainment). 2001. Dvd.

Bauer, Y. *American Jewry and the Holocaust: The American Jewish Joint Distribution Committee, 1939-1945*. Michigan: Wayne State University Press. June 1981.

———. Jewish Baranowice in the Holocaust. *Yad Vashem Studies, 31,* 95-152. 2003.

Berger, A. *Second Generation Voices*. New York: Syracuse University Press. 2001.

Berman, D. A Prayer Book's Journey. *Yad Vashem*. Retrieved from http://www1. yadvashem.org/yv/en/remembrance/names/pdf/magazine55.pdf 2010.

Bodian, M. *Hebrews of the Portuguese Nation: Conversos and Community in Early Modern Amsterdam*: Indiana University Press 1999.

Breitman, R. *American Refugee Policy and European Jewry, 1933-1945*. Indiana: Indiana University Press. 1 Jan. 1988.

Bishop, C., & Joly, J. *Twenty & Ten*. London: Puffin. 30 March 1978.

Brachfeld, S. *A Gift of Life: The Deportation and the Rescue of the Jews in Occupied Belgium (1940-1944)*. Herzliya: Institute for the Research on Belgian Judaism. 2007.

Budapest. *United States Holocaust Memorial Museum*. Retrieved from http://www. ushmm.org/wlc/en/article.php?ModuleId=10005264 . 1 April 2010.

Callil, C. *Bad Faith*. New York: Knopf. 2006.

Carrol, J. *Constantine's Sword: The Church and the Jews: A History*. Massachusetts:Houghton Mifflin Harcourt. 10 January 2001.

Castle Zuylen, Utrecht. *Castles*. info. Retrieved from http://www.castles.info/netherlands/zuylen/2005.

Cholawsky, S. *The Jews of Bielorussia during World War II*. Amsterdam: Harwood Academic Publishers. 1998.

Cohn, S.w.a.Sara Lea Needle *Bella's Story, from Pogrom to Holocaust*. Readers Theatre. 4 January 2011.

Cohn, S. N. *Holocaust Research Project*. UCF College of Education. Retrieved from www.education.ucf.edu/holocaust. 1 January 2010.

Commune de Quaregnon. Retrieved June 2010. http://www.quaregnon.be/.

Davies, N., & Polonsky, A. (Eds.). *Jews in Eastern Poland and the USSR, 1939-46*. New York: St. Martin's Press. 1991.

Dean, M. *Collaboration in the Holocaust: Crimes of the Local Police in Belorussia and Ukraine, 1941-41.* London: Palgrave Macmillan. 2000.

De Rosnay, T. *Sarah's Key*. New York: St Martin's Press. 12 June 2007.

Diamond Trade and Industry. *Jewish Virtual Library*. 2008.Retrieved from http:// www.jewishvirtuallibrary.org/jsource/judaica/ejud_0002_0005_0_05194.html.

Dobroszycki, L., & Gurock, J. S. (Eds.). *The Holocaust in the Soviet Union. Studies and Sources on the Destruction of the Jews in the Nazi-Occupied Territories of the USSR, 1941-1945*. New York: ME Sharpe. 1993.

Dr. Lucile Baroness Tuyll Serooskerken United Peace Foundation (UPF) Retrieved http://www.upf-nederland.nl/July 2010.

Dubno. *Jewish Virtual Library*. Retrieved from http://www.jewishvirtuallibrary.org/ jsource/judaica/ejud_0002_0006_0_05436.html. January 2008.

*Dubno Memorial Book* Hebrew & Yiddish. Jerusalem: Yad Vashem. 2006.

Duffy, Peter. *The Bielski Brothers*. NY: Harper Perennial. 2004.

Dutch Jewish Psychiatric Hospital Enjoys Support of Royal Family. *Chabad*. 9 December 2008. Retrieved from http://www.chabad.org/news/article_cdo/aid/784936/ jewish/Jewish-Hospital-Grows-in-Netherlands.htm.

Dutch West India Company. *Wikipedia*. Retrieved from http://en.wikipedia.org/wiki/ Dutch_West_India_Company. 27 August 2010.

*Echoes and Reflections: A Multimedia Curriculum on the Holocaust* Anti-Defamation League, USC Shoah Foundation & Yad Vashem, Jerusalem: Yad Vashem Martyrs' and Heroes' Remembrance Authority. 2005.

Eliach, Y. *There Once was a World: A 900-Year Chronicle of the Shtetl of Eishyshok.* New York: Little Brown & Co. October 1998.

Elson, J., & Levy, D. S. History: Did FDR do enough? *TIME.* Retrieved from http://www.time.com/time/magazine/article/0,9171,980552,00.html. 3 August 2010.

Epstein, H. *Children of the Holocaust.* New York: Penguin. 1988.

Ettinger, L. *From the Lida Ghetto to the Bielski Partisans.* Washington D.C.: United States Holocaust Memorial Museum. December 1984.

Ettinger, S. Volhynia. *Jewish Virtual Library.* 2008.Retrieved from http://www.jewishvirtuallibrary.org/jsource/judaica/ejud_0002_0020_0_20487.html.

Fink, I. *The Tenth Man.* In F. Prose, & M. Levine (Eds.), *A Scrap of Time* (pp. 103-115). Jerusalem: Yad Vashem. 1999.

Frank, Anne , Frank, Otto H.; Pressler, Mirjam eds. (in Dutch) *Het Achterhuis . 1947. [The Diary of a Young Girl—The Definitive Edition]* Massotty, Susan (translation) Doubleday. 1995.

Franklin Delano Roosevelt. United States Holocaust Memorial Museum. Retrieved from http://www.ushmm.org/wlc/en/article.php?ModuleId=10007411. 1 April 2010.

Frojimovics, K., Pusztai, V., & Strbik, A. *Jewish Budapest: Monuments, Rites, History.* New York: Central European University Press. 1999.

Gelman, C. *Do Not Go Gentle: A Memoir of Jewish Resistance in Poland, 1941-1945.* Connecticut: Archon Books. 1989.

Ghitis, O. A Brief History of the Jewish Settlement of Sosua, Dominican Republic. Centro Israelita de la República Dominicana. Retrieved from http://www.kosherdelight.com/DominicanRepublicOisikiJewishSettlementSosui.shtml. 2010.

Gilbert, M. *The Holocaust: The Jewish Tragedy.* Glasgow: William Collins. 1986.

Gitelman, Z. Y. *Jewish nationality and soviet politics.* NJ: Princeton University Press. 1972.

Goddet, J. The track that died of shame. *Procycling.* 2002.

Greenfeld, H. *After the Holocaust.* NY: Harper Collins. 2001.

Gross, J. T. *Revolution from Abroad: The Soviet Conquest of Poland's Western Ukraine and Western Belorussia.* New Jersey: Princeton University Press. 1988.

Gross, J. T. *Neighbors: The Destruction of the Jewish Community in Jedwabne, Poland.* New Jersey: Princeton University Press. 2001.

Gruber, R. *Exodus 1947: The Ship that Launched a Nation.* New York: Crown. 1 October 1999.

Gutman, Y., & Krakowski, S. *Unequal Victims: Poles and Jews During World War Two.* New York: Holocaust Library. 1986.

Haberer, E. The German police and genocide in Belorussia, 1941-1944. Part II: "The second sweep": Gendarmerie killings of Jews and Gypsies on January, 22, 1942. *Journal of Genocide Research, 3(2),* 207. June 2001.

———. The German police and genocide in Belorussia, 1941-1944. Part I: Police deployment and Nazi genocidal directives. *Journal of Genocide Research, 3(1),* 17. March 2001. Retrieved from http://web.ebscohost.com.ezproxy.lib.ucf.edu/

ehost/pdf?vid=5&hid=106&sid=3025b77c-02cc-467e-ab1f-017bfbfedf65%
40sessionmgr112.

———. The German police in Belorussia, 1941-1944, part III: Methods of genocide and the motives of German police compliance. *Journal of Genocide Research, 3(3),* 391. November 2001.

Harkawi, S. A., & Katzenlson, L. Pruzana in three encyclopedias. *Rootsweb.* Retrieved from http://freepages.genealogy.rootsweb.ancestry.com/~cpsa/pruzany/pruzhist.htm . 28 October 2009.

Hartman, J. J., & Krochmal, J. (Eds.). *I Remember Every Day... The Fates of the Jews of Przemysl during World War II.* Michigan: Remembrance and Reconciliation. 2002.

*Help for the Jews: a ray of hope, Comite de Defense des Juifs*-CDJ .The Jewish Museum of Deportation & Resistance. Retrieved from http://www.cicb.be/en/help. htm#CDJENG. 28 August 2010.

Hilberg, Raul. *Perpetrators, Victims, Bystanders the Jewish Catastrophe 1933-1945.* NY: Harper Collins. 1992. History of the Jews in the Netherlands. *Wikpedia.* Retrieved from http://en.wikipedia.org/wiki/History_of_the_Jews_in_the_Netherlands. 11 June 2010.

———. *The Destruction of the European Jews* (3rd ). London: Yale University Press. 2003.

———. *Perpetrators, Victims, Bystanders: Jewish Catastrophe 1933-1945.* New York: Harper Collins. 1992.

History of the Jews in the Dominican Republic. *Wikipedia.* Retrieved from http://en.wikipedia.org/wiki/History_of_the_Jews_in_the_Dominican_Republic 23 August 2010.

Holocaust Testimonies. 2010. *PolishJews.org.* Retrieved from http://www.polish jews.org/shoahtts/019.htm. 1992.

Huneke, D *The Moses of Rovno; Fritz Graebe.* Dodd Meade.1985.

Hungary Before the German Occupation. United States Holocaust Memorial Museum. Retrieved from http://www.ushmm.org/wlc/en/article.php?ModuleId=10005457. 1 April 2010.

Hungary After the German Occupation. *United States Holocaust Memorial Museum.* Retrieved from http://www.ushmm.org/wlc/en/article.php?ModuleId=10005458 . 1 April 2010.

I Survived the 20th Century Holocaust: Part I. *Holocaust Survivors and Remembrance Project.* Retrieved from http://isurvived.org/TOC-I.html#The_Netherlands.2010.

Jacobsen, R. *Rescued Images: Memories of a Childhood in Hiding.* NY: Mikaya Press. 2001.

Kamen, H. *The Spanish Inquisition: A Historical Revision.* London: Yale Univ. Press. 1997.

Kamins, T. . *The Complete Jewish Guide to France.* NY: St.Martin Griffin. September 2001.

Kaplan, M. *Dominican Haven: The Jewish Refugee Settlement in Sosua, 1940-1945.* New York: Museum of Jewish Heritage. 15 February 2008.

Katz, E. B. *Our Tomorrows Never Came.* New York: Fordham University Press. 2000.

Kirchwey, F. Caribbean Refuge. The Nation, in the papers of Cecilia Razovsky. 13April 1940. American Jewish Historical Society. http://findingaids.cjh. org/?pID=109184.

Krell, R. Child survivors of the Holocaust: Forty years later. *Journal American Academy Child Psychiatry.* 2005.

Land-Weber, E. *To Save a Life: Stories Of Holocaust Rescue.* Illinois: University of Illinois Press. 2000.

Lazarus (Leo) Fuld Where Can I Go? Song Lyrics O. Strock & Music S. Korn-tuer http://wn.com/The_king_of_Yiddish_Music_Leo_Fuld__Where_can_I_go?_Wo_ Ahin_soll_Ich_Geh%27n?

Lecomte, J.P. *Le temoignage chretien du Protestantsisme borain sous l'occupation allemande pendant la seconde guerre mondiale 1939-1945.* Belgium: Universitaire de Theologie Protestante de Bruxelles. 1981.

Leo Fuld. *Wikipedia.* Retrieved from http://en.wikipedia.org/wiki/Leo_Fuld . 24 July 2010.

Levendel, I. *Not the Germans Alone: A Son's Search for the Truth of Vichy.* Illinois: Northwestern University Press. 21 May 2001.

Levine, K. *Hana's Suitcase.* Illinois: Albert Whitman & Company. 1 January 2003.

Levitan, M. *Through Hell and Back.* Canada. 1953.

List of Dutch Jews. *Wikipedia.* Retrieved from http://en.wikipedia.org/wiki/List_of_ Dutch_Jews. 18 August 2010.

Maerten, F. *Du Murmure Au Grondement. La Resistance politique et ideologique dans la province du Hainaut pendant la Seconde Guerre Mondiale ( Mai 1940-1944 ) Analectes d'Histoire du Hainaut.*tome 7-Volume III ,Collection Publiee par Hannonia. Belgium: Mons, 1999.

Medoff, R., & Bittinger, C. How Grace Coolidge Almost Saved Anne Frank. The David S. Wyman Institute for Holocaust Studies. Retrieved from http://www. wymaninstitute.org/articles/2007-3-coolidge.php. 3 August 2010.

Memorial Books. *United States Holocaust Memorial Museum.* Retrieved from http:// www.ushmm.org/research/library/family/books/#S. 2010.

Mendelsohn, D. *The Lost: A Search for Six of Six Million.* New York: Harper Perennial. 2007.

Mokotoff, G., Sack, S., & Sharon, A. *Where Once We Walked: A Guide to the Jewish Communities Destroyed in the Holocaust.* New Jersey: Avotaynu. May 1991.

Moya Pons, F. *The Dominican Republic: A National History.* New Jersey: Markus Wiener Publishers. 1 May 1998.

Nachmany-Gafny, E. Dividing Hearts: The Removal of Jewish Children from Gentile Families in Poland in the Immediate Post-Holocaust Years. Jerusalem: Yad Vashem. 2009.

Nineteen Forty-Two to Nineteen Forty-Four. *The Jewish Museum of Deportation & Resistance.* Retrieved from http://www.cicb.be/en/period3.htm. 28 August 2010.

Oreck, A. The Virtual Jewish History Tour: Belgium. *Jewish Virtual Library.* Retrieved from http://www.jewishvirtuallibrary.org/jsource/vjw/Belgium.html .2009.

Pakula, A. J. (Director). *Sophie's Choice* [Film]. (Available from Incorporated Television Company). 1982.

Paul, M. Neighbours On The Eve Of The Holocaust: Polish-Jewish Relations In Soviet-Occupied Eastern Poland, 1939-1941. 13 December 2009. *The Polish Educational Foundation in North America.* Retrieved from http://www.electronicmuseum.ca/Poland-WW2/ethnic_minorities_occupation/jews.html.

Polanski, R. (Director). *The Pianist* [Dvd]. (Available from Universal Studios). 2002.

Portuguese Synagogue Amsterdam. *Amsterdam.info.* Retrieved from http://www. amsterdam.info/portuguese-synagogue/. 2010.

Priewe, J., & Priewe, C. *Vom Schattenland Ins Tropenlicht Ein Lebenswegbeschreibung.* Cabarete, Dominican Republic: Publisher.2006.

Rapoport, S. *Yesterdays and then Tommorows: Holocaust Anthology of Testimonies and Readings.* The International School for Holocaust Studies, Jerusalem, Israel. 2002.

Reich, H. *The First and Final Nightmare of Sonia Reich: A Son's Memoir.* New York: PublicAffairs. 13 June 2006.

Refugees, The Exodus at Haifa. *Time International.* 28 July 1947.

Research and Education. *Allgenerations.* Retrieved from www.allgenerations.org. 2010.

*Resistance.* Jerusalem: Yad Vashem, Israel. 2004.

Robinson, M. Richard Bradley, Escape from Stalag VIIIB, Part 4—Capture. *BBC.* 4 January 2010.Retrieved from http://www.bbc.co.uk/ww2peopleswar/stories/34/a7212034.shtml.

Roorda, E. *The Dictator Next Door: The Good Neighbor Policy and the Trujillo Regime in the Dominican Republic, 1930-1945.* North Carolina: Duke University Press. October 1998.

Romanovsky, D. Soviet jews under Nazi occupation in northeastern Belarus and western Russia. In Z. Gitelman (Ed.), *Bitter legacy: Confronting the holocaust in the USSR* (pp. 230). Indianapolis, IN: Indiana University Press. 1997.

Rudomin, A. (Director). *Day of Wrath* [Dvd]. (Available MGM Home Entertainment). 2006.

Sagas, E. Race & Politics in the Dominican Republic. Florida: University Press of Florida. 21 April 2000.

Schoenfeld, J. *Holocaust Memoirs: Jews in the Lwow Ghetto, the Janowski Concentration Camp, and as Deportees in Siberia.* New Jersey: Ktav Publishing House. 1985.

Shoes on the Danube,Gyula Pauer Memorial . 2005. *Wikipedia.* Retrieved from http://en.wikipedia.org/wiki/Shoes_on_the_Danube_Promenade.18 September 2010.

Shyovitz, D. The Virtual Jewish History Tour: Netherlands. *The Jewish Virtual Library.* 2010. Retrieved fromhttp://www.jewishvirtuallibrary.org/jsource/vjw/netherlands.html.

Siedlce. *Wikipedia.* Retrieved from http://en.wikipedia.org/wiki/Siedlce. 30 July 2010.

*Siedlce Image Gallery* [Photograph]. Retrieved from: http://www.holocaustresearch-project.org/ghettos/siedlce%20gallery/Sidelce%20Deportations.html.

*Siedlce Ghetto. Deathcamps.org.* 28 September 2006.Retrieved from http://www. deathcamps.org/occupation/siedlce%20ghetto.html.

Slot Zuylen Castle, a unique experience. *Slot* Zuylen. Retrieved from http://www. slotzuylen.nl/english/. 2010.

Smilovitsky, L. A demographic profile of the Jews in Belorussia from the pre-war time to the post-war time. *Journal of Genocide Research, 5(1),* 117. March 2003.

*Sosua: An American Jewish Experiment.* Jewish Virtual Library. Retrieved from http://www.jewishvirtuallibrary.org/jsource/Holocaust/sosua1.html . 2010.

Sosua: A Refuge for Jews in the Dominican Republic. *Museum of Jewish Heritage.* Retrieved from http://www.mjhnyc.org/final/documents/SosuaTG3.pdf. 2009.

Spanish Inquisition. *Wikipedia.* Retrived from http://en.wikipedia.org/wiki/Spanish_Inquisition. 28 August 2008.

Spiegelman, A. *The Complete Maus: A Survivor's Tale.* New York: Pantheon. 19 November 1996.

Spielberg, S. (Director). *Schindler's List* [Film]. (Available from Universal Pictures). 15 December 1993.

SS Exodus.*Wikipedia.* Retrieved from http://en.wikipedia.org/wiki/SS_Exodus. 29 August 2010.

Steinfeld, I. *How was it Humanly Possible? A Study of Perpetrators and Bystanders During the Holocaust.* Jerusalem: Yad Vashem. 2002.

*Strzemieszyce* .2010. Retrieved from http://www.jewishgen.org/yizkor/Strzemieszyce/Strzemieszyce.html.

Taub, H., & Kafka, H. (Producer). *Sosua, a Haven in the Caribbean* [Dvd]. (Available from Sosua-Sol Productions). 2006.

Tec, N. *Defiance: The Bielski Partisans.* New York: Oxford University Press. 1993.

———. *When Light Pierced the Darkness: Christian Rescue of Jews in Nazi-Occupied Poland.* New York: Oxford University Press. 1986.

The Earthenware Factory of Wasmuel. *La Faiencerie de Wasmuel.* 28 August 2010. Retrieved from http://www.faienceriedewasmuel-macollection.com/historique%20 anglais.htm.

The Einsatzgruppen. *Holocaust Research Project.* Retrieved from http://www.holocaustresearchproject.org/einsatz/index.html .2007.

The Portuguese Synagogue. *Esnoga.* Retrieved from http://www.esnoga.nl/. 2010.

The Righteous Among the Nations. *Yad Vashem.* 2010. Retrieved from http://www1. yadvashem.org/yv/en/remembrance/multimedia.asp.

Treblinka. *United States Holocaust Memorial Museum.* Retrieved from http://www. ushmm.org/wlc/en/article.php?ModuleId=1000519 .1 April 2010.

Tuyll. *Wikipedia.* Retrieved from http://en.wikipedia.org/wiki/Tuyll .27 August 2010.

Uris, L. *The Exodus.* New York: Bantam Dell. 1 October 1983.

Utgof, V. In search of national support: Belorussian refugees in World War I and People's Republic of Belarus. In N. Baron & P. Gatrell (Eds.), *Homelands: War, population, and statehood in Eastern Europe and Russia, 1918-1924* (pp. 53). London, England: Anthem Press. 2004.

*Volhynia* Dec.2009.Retrieved from http://www.Jewishvirtual library.org/.

Van Tuyll Van Serooskerken Eighteenth Century. 2010. Retrieved from: http://www. worldlingo.com/ma/enwiki/en/Tuyll#Eighteenth_century.

Voltaire. *Candide.* New York:Bedford/St. Martin's.15 September 1998.

Weiner, R. The Virtual Jewish History Tour: Budapest. *Jewish Virtual Library.* 2009. Retrieved fromhttp://www.jewishvirtuallibrary.org/jsource/vjw/Budapest.html.

Westerbork. *United States Holocaust Memorial Museum.* Retrieved from http://www. ushmm.org/wlc/en/article.php?ModuleId=10005217. April 1 2010.

Westerbork Transit Camp (Holland). *JewishGen.* Retrieved from http://www.jewishgen.org/ForgottenCamps/Camps/WestEng.html. 2010.

Westerkerk. *Wikipedia.* Retrieved from http://en.wikipedia.org/wiki/Westerkerk. 1 September 2010.

Weiner, R. The Virtual Jewish Library Tour: France. *Jewish Virtual Library.* Retrieved from http://www.jewishvirtuallibrary.org/jsource/vjw/France.html. 2009.

Weiner, R. The Virtual Jewish History Tour: Poland. *Jewish Virtual Library.* Retrieved from http://www.jewishvirtuallibrary.org/jsource/vjw/Poland.html. 2010.

Wells, A. *Tropical Zion: General Trujillo, FDR & the Jews of Sosua.* North Carolina: Duke University Press. 2009.

Wiesel, E. *Night.* New York: Hill & Wang. September 1960.

Wyman, D. *The Abandonment of the Jews: America & the Holocaust 1941-1945.* New York: New Press. 1998.

Zapruder, A. *Salvaged Pages: Young Writers' Diaries of the Holocaust.* Connecticut: Yale: University Press. 1 April 2002.

Zaprudnik, J. *Belarus: At a Crossroads in History.* Colorado: Westview Press. 1993.

Zucker, B. *In Search of Refuge: Jews & the US Consuls in Nazi Germany 1933-1941.* New York: American Jewish Historical Society. 1 September 2001.

Zwick, E. (Director). *Defiance* [Dvd]. (Available from Paramount Vantage, 555 Melrose Ave., Chevalier Bldg., 2nd Fl. Los Angeles, CA 90038). 2008.

# Index

NOTE: Page numbers in *italic* indicate photos